# RAW

# RAW

## MY 100% GRADE-A, UNFILTERED, INSIDE LOOK AT SPORTS

## COLIN COWHERD

G

GALLERY BOOKS

New York   London   Toronto   Sydney   New Delhi

# G

Gallery Books
An Imprint of Simon & Schuster, Inc.
1230 Avenue of the Americas
New York, NY 10020

First Gallery Books hardcover edition October 2015

GALLERY BOOKS and colophon are registered trademarks
of Simon & Schuster, Inc.

For information about special discounts for bulk purchases,
please contact Simon & Schuster Special Sales at 1-866-506-1949
or business@simonandschuster.com.

The Simon & Schuster Speakers Bureau can bring authors
to your live event. For more information or to book an event,
contact the Simon & Schuster Speakers Bureau at 1-866-248-3049
or visit our website at www.simonspeakers.com.

Interior design by Davina Mock-Maniscalco

Manufactured in the United States of America

10   9   8   7   6   5   4   3   2   1

Library of Congress Cataloging-in-Publication Data is available.

ISBN 978-1-5011-0519-7
ISBN 978-1-5011-0520-3 (ebook)

*To the mom who taught me right from wrong*

# INTRODUCTION

**O**NCE UPON A TIME, you could open a newspaper or watch a television news channel with an open mind. You weren't immediately informed—by story placement, headline, or tone—which direction the media outlet in question was leaning politically. Believe it or not, you were trusted to consume the news and reach your own conclusions. If you're in your twenties or early thirties, you're just going to have to trust me on this one.

There was also a time, lo those many years ago, when local sportscasters didn't automatically assume the default position of supporting the local team or the local star on every single controversial issue. Again, you younger people are going to have to take my word for it: local news crews didn't always gear up in the home team's cap and jersey every time the heroes made the postseason.

# INTRODUCTION

Opinions have always been part of the sports media, dating back to the days when the big-city columnist was a celebrity on a par with the All-Star centerfielder. Understandably, the volume of opinion has increased, along with the number of outlets. Technology and availability of content have created more informed consumers, and they demand more than a bland regurgitation of how yesterday's runs scored. You know the *who* and the *what*, so now you demand the *why*.

But something important and unfortunate has happened along the way. I'm not sure how it came about, or who is to blame, but the media personality who pulls no punches has become an endangered species. It's been a gradual creep for more than a decade, but it hit me directly over the head as I followed the coverage of the Tom Brady/New England Patriots "Deflategate" story.

Honestly, it was nothing short of jaw-dropping to witness the performance of the Boston media during the entire episode. In one of America's most educated cities, with perhaps our nation's richest sports history, local outlets transformed themselves into pom-pom waving, jersey-wearing, fist-pumping superfans. From the venerable pages of the *Boston Globe* to the toxic airwaves of WEEI Radio, it was a hazmat spill of homerism.

Where to start? It was juvenile, pandering, and irrational—the triple crown of awful. I felt like I was reading *The Onion*, or listening to someone read it to me. But instead of purposefully satirical headlines—"CIA Realizes It's Been Using Black Hi-Liters All These Years" or "Members of Twisted Sister Now

Willing to Take It"—the *Boston Herald* was unintentionally bewildering.

Maybe one of the headline writers was simply overworked—or better yet, drowning in gin-and-tonics—when he decided to drop "Why Do They Hate Us?" atop the tabloid's front page, hovering menacingly over four Lombardi trophies. For starters, you persecuted souls, how's this for an answer: "Because your increasingly greasy football operation tried to convince us that the use of the word 'deflator' in texts was actually used to describe dietary goals."

But is this what we want now? Do we want a media that makes us comfortable by placating and pandering to the dimmest and least discerning? Are we sending messages, through ratings or readership, that we're all about the lowest common denominator? Do we really want media that pats us on the head the way Dad did to comfort us after a Little League loss?

I'm also sensing a second, equally disturbing trend in the media, but I think I'm going to amend that description—because using the word *trend* implies that it is temporary. In this case, I'm not sure, so I will call the following a disturbing reality: take a side, regardless of evidence to the contrary, and never, ever be willing to budge.

I noticed this—an invasive and destructive algae growing in the media pond—when Conan O'Brien was handed Jay Leno's *Tonight Show* slot on NBC. The media viewed Leno as a workaholic grinder who politicked his way into the prime slot that was expected to be the domain of David Letterman. Leno's comedy was viewed by coastal elites as less urbane than either Dave's or Conan's. The problem for the media was this: Leno clobbered both in the ratings, even though the coverage led you to believe the exact opposite.

The media had made up their minds, though, and there was no going back. Leno was not funny, and Conan was seizure-inducing, roll-off-the-couch-and-spit-Mountain-Dew hilarious.

This is the new normal for the media, not just an occasional off-speed pitch meant to keep the audience on its toes. In sports, the latest Leno-level target (threat level: orange) is NFL commissioner Roger Goodell. The son of a senator, a man who captained three high school sports teams as a senior and would later earn a degree in economics from a well-respected private college, is officially the least competent man in professional sports.

Forget everything that came before. Forget that former commissioner Paul Tagliabue, a dry leader but a revered negotiator, offered a young Goodell control of everything from new stadium projects to business operations, and he passed with flying colors. Forget that thirty-two team owners, among the top businessmen in America, voted for Goodell almost unanimously more than a decade ago and handed him one of the most coveted jobs in sports. Despite these facts, according to the media mob, Goodell is now incapable of running anything more complex than a do-it-yourself car wash. There's no question Goodell is imperfect, but he's far from incompetent.

The root of the criticism is the idea that Goodell is too powerful. So despite record profits, record ratings, and the creation of an undeniably safer game compared with his first day on the job, Goodell is a man who arrives at the office without realizing he forgot to wear pants.

So welcome, ladies and gentlemen, to the wonderful world of media. Trustworthiness has plummeted, and for good reason. Opinions from formerly respected sources are now presented either to reaffirm our own opinions—coddling, in essence—or to condemn those in power who dare to hold positions that run counter to our beliefs.

The first sportscaster to make me think was Howard Cosell. Sure, he got bitter at the end, but it was his utter disregard for public approval that still sticks with me today. His philosophy was as direct as one of his on-air sermons: be harsh if it's called for, and be prepared to be hated if it unveils an uncomfortable truth.

Don't mollify—ever. Crucify with discretion. Understand there is no precise answer to every argument. Fans deserve both nuance and bluntness.

I'm ready to deliver all of the above. You with me?

# THE SADDEST SUPERHERO

**I** **WAS LIKE MOST KIDS.** I woke up on Saturday mornings to watch cartoons. A handful of them couldn't be missed. *Scooby-Doo, Where Are You!* was strangely addictive despite featuring a talking dog, four teenagers who never changed their clothes, and the exact same ending to every episode: a thwarted villain saying, "I would have pulled this off without you meddling kids!" There was also *Jonny Quest*, an adventure series where two families traveled the globe finding evil, like the one time when they discovered the giant spider whose eye was a camera sending pictures back to the bad guy Dr. Zin. I don't want to go too deeply into the details, but that shit was *real*.

I followed the path of most boys, seduced into the shows that chronicled the exploits of crime fighters and superheroes. Spider-Man, Batman, the Green Lantern, Plastic Man—they all

1

had a place in my heart. I would try to decipher in my head which one of them I would choose in a battle to the death. I would assess from all angles, analyzing strengths and weaknesses, sort of an early sabermetric version of advanced-metric cartoon analysis.

As I've aged, I've come up with a superhero that would defeat them all. He isn't very big, and he probably can't lift so much as a couch without the help of several other people. There's no X-ray vision, although there's a chance he could be a recent recipient of Lasik surgery. His speed, even among the rest of his out-of-shape friends, is pedestrian.

And yet this guy's magic is undeniable. He can stop any person—even any group—in his tracks. He can petrify even the most powerful among us; he is unable to stop a steaming locomotive but perfectly capable of creating corporate chaos with just a few well-placed words. Even the other superheroes don't dare cross him.

Who is this unmasked man? How can someone be so powerful and mundane at the same time?

Let me introduce you to Claiming Racism Man.

The first thing you need to know is that he doesn't need proof. He can work his magic without the benefit of evidence—no repeated actions caught on tape or in writing necessary. He can claim racism against a company without poring over recent hiring practices or disputed firings. No, the source of this superhero's power comes from the overwhelming randomness and impulsivity of his words. If you make a claim that doesn't fit his political leanings, you're in danger of being targeted.

It's a bird, it's a plane—wait, he's not up in the sky at all. In fact, he's writing on a blog, of all things.

*It's . . .*

*Claiming Racism Man.*

If you think I'm exaggerating the power of race and the irrational way in which we treat intentions that are inherently reasonable, I'll offer you a quick and easy example.

Starbucks launched a campaign in early 2015 called "Race Together," and it was intended to decrease racial injustice and bring a better understanding of the issues affecting people of all races. Baristas, if they so desired, could add the hashtag #RaceTogether on the side of cups in hopes of sparking discussion—or even simple consideration—of the issues facing minorities. The idea was to plant the idea that no matter who you are or where you came from, we're all in this together.

There was absolutely nothing sinister at work here.

Baristas weren't instructed to take your order and proclaim, "I see you ordered another *vanilla* latte today. Isn't it about time for some *dark* roast, if you know what I mean?" There were no reports of baristas holding out a customer's Breakfast Blend and refusing to hand it over until the customer came up with the right answer to the question "Do you think Oprah got hosed at the Oscars?"

Oh, but you wouldn't know that from the outcry. Within a few days, we had ourselves a veritable firestorm over two voluntary words on paper coffee cups—words that, frankly, would have little or no impact on the systemic issues that create the kind of racial tension that results in the death of someone like Trayvon Martin or Michael Brown.

Nobody can deny that racism exists here, or nearly anywhere. Even among the better educated, there is closeted racism, or—in the case of the most affluent among us—walk-in-closeted racism.

But how did a simple campaign seeking potential civilized discourse on the subject pick up so much momentum, not to mention unmitigated scorn?

I'll tell you why: because we're so petrified of being called a racist or forever labeled a racist that even thoughtful discourse can lead to unintentional misinterpretation or manipulation. It's better to keep your damned mouth shut than to end up saying something that might inadvertently end with you having an exit interview in human resources forty-five minutes after you opened your mouth.

Claiming Racism Man has a posse behind him, too, making him even more powerful. The racial police, often working behind the scenes in support of Claiming Racism Man, feel that they—and only they—have the superior intellect to discuss any aspect of the topic. Really? Is the club *that* exclusive? We have governors and presidents who make wide-ranging economic decisions affecting hundreds of millions of people without having a single professional career in their backgrounds, and yet discussions of race—the act of merely talking about the topic—should be reserved for a chosen few?

The beauty of Claiming Racism Man is his dexterity. He has

an amazing ability to twist and reconfigure someone's words to unearth the hidden meanings that lie within the most innocuous comments. You want a concrete example? You're in luck.

My friend Max Bretos, a *SportsCenter* anchor at ESPN and one of the nicest humans I've ever known, used the phrase "chink in his armor" to describe a bad game by former New York Knicks point guard Jeremy Lin. Bretos's comment came as Lin's incredible surge of popularity—known as "Linsanity"—briefly dominated the New York sports scene in 2012. Claiming Racism Man leaped into the manufactured controversy, and when it was over, Bretos was handed a thirty-day suspension.

Such is the power of Claiming Racism Man that nobody cared about the origins of the phrase, which dates back to the fifteenth century and has absolutely no connection to the Asian racial slur. Let me repeat: it is an innocuous phrase, no more demeaning to Asians than saying "That's his Achilles heel" is demeaning to everyone of Greek descent.

And such is the power—excuse me, *super*power—of Claiming Racism Man that it didn't seem to matter that Bretos is married to an Asian woman. His children are Asian, and somehow he's not only a racist but a racist *against Asians?* Go, CRM, go.

When the issue is literally black and white, African Americans often feel that Caucasians don't understand the black experience. That may be true, and in many cases it is undeniably true, but how can anyone learn anything without discussing it?

*Racism*—the word, not the act itself—is now a weapon used viciously and cavalierly without discretion or proof. It's sure to get clicks on blogs and create debates on cable sports and news shows, but it has also become tired and overused. It has one purpose—*Gotcha!*—and it has reached the point where I become cynical before I even know the details of the story behind the claim.

In the end, Claiming Racism Man uses his power to simplify a complex topic, turning it into a seventh-grade name-calling contest rather than an attempt at civic improvement. Instead of discussing policies that are institutionally racist and have generational consequences for minorities—housing discrimination, for instance, or economic redlining—we yell and point and get all worked up over isolated sentences that have no real impact beyond defaming a single and often powerless person.

I should probably wrap this up now, because I think I can hear the footsteps of Claiming Racism Man as he closes in on me. It sounds dangerous, I know, but I'd love to sit down with him and examine my opinions—the ones he derides so angrily. But, alas, we know how this game works. I'm not black enough. I'm not smart enough.

Claiming Racism Man's power is exceeded only by one other quality: his ability to annoy. It's one of the reasons Spider-Man no longer calls him a friend.

# ARROGANCE
## IS CONFIDENCE
### WITHOUT A FILTER.

# ONE ORDER OF GAIN, PLEASE HOLD THE PAIN

**A**RROYO HIGH SCHOOL, sandwiched between a couple of small parks in San Bernardino, is just one of roughly 4,500 California high schools you might come across as you drive past on the interstate. In other words, you probably wouldn't even notice it unless you were looking for it.

But that all changed in the third week of January, when an atrocity took place at Arroyo High that made my radio audience angry and defiant. Incidents like the one that took place that infamous Tuesday night should never be allowed. We all deserve better, and the school needs to be investigated and monitored from this moment forward. Trust me when I tell you it was all very forceful and self-righteous. These folks simply weren't going to stand for this kind of crap anymore.

So what happened, you ask?

The Arroyo girls' basketball team really clobbered the girls' team from Bloomington, about thirty minutes away. Nobody on the losing team was injured, and the girls from Bloomington were bused back to their school that night, where their parents waited to take them home, presumably for a snack and maybe a little homework before bed. According to school records, attendance wasn't abnormally low the following day or week.

The score was 161–2. Uniquely lopsided, yes, but if it had ended up 86–8, would the losing team have felt better about itself? When does a blowout go beyond the realm of the uncomfortable and reach psychologically damaging heights? Do kids get teased in the hallway for losing 76–14 but hear nothing if it's 68–19?

My takeaways that day on the radio, amid the clamor of the outraged, were unpopular. I can distill it all into three words: get over it.

First, blowouts are unavoidable at the youth level. Unlike pro sports, where things like salary caps, free-agent guidelines, and revenue sharing tend to get in the way, youth sports are as uneven as the affluence of any given community. Some schools go all-in, building college-sized arenas and football stadiums on the backs of willing taxpayers and wealthy donors. Other schools need car washes and bake sales to generate enough revenue for baseball bats and barbells.

Trust me, blowouts are happening Monday through Saturday in a zip code near you. And even though most—no, let's say nearly all—youth coaches have a sense of fairness and an understanding of the appropriate climate, there are also schmucks in every district or youth league. It's the reality of youth sports, and we've all endured it. There's no reason to lose any sleep over it.

Second, I'd like to make a point that touches on an uncomfortable truth, one that most parents don't want to acknowledge. We want our kids to display a certain amount of grit and fortitude. We want them to fight through the hard parts and store away a supply of toughness that will drive them through life when things turn rough. But something weird happens in the process: most of us, me included, aren't always comfortable with what it takes to get there.

We want the gain without the pain. It rarely works that way.

I see a similar debate with our current need for personal security. Americans want to retain all their personal information without a snooping, drone-like presence hovering overhead. We are often outraged by a government that would monitor some of our activities, but we're the first ones to vote a local or national politician out of office if he was ever linked to a policy that endangers our family's safety from domestic or international threats.

Professionals who specialize in family dynamics acknowledge the existence of traits like middle-child syndrome, in which birth order can affect the personality of children and adults more than external forces do. What I'm saying is that siblings can share the same parents, the same DNA, the same school, and sit down to dinner as a family nightly, and yet be opposites in terms of personality. One is shy and withdrawn, while the other, despite sharing a bedroom for eighteen years, is outgoing and exuberant. My point is this: we control our kid's personalities much less than we would like to believe. Barring any physical abuse, most kids will probably turn out okay.

I'd go so far as to say that humiliating sports losses may be more reliable character builders than the ceaseless flow of compliments and bubble-wrap protection parents use to make sure their adorable little Tiffany isn't exposed to any of society's harsher elements.

Is it merely coincidence that few professional athletes come from wealthy parents? Wealth would obviously confer nutritional and training benefits from an early age, but the vast majority of the millionaires you watch on television grew up closer to the poverty line than to the country club. It's doubtful that the rage with which the Seattle Seahawks' Marshawn Lynch runs has its roots in private tennis lessons at summer camp.

I have no doubt those girls from Bloomington were bummed after losing by more than 150 points, but I'd wager they would be much more heartbroken had their boyfriends dumped them or if they'd flunked a French midterm. It's unlikely they got on the bus that night thinking they were going up to Arroyo to lay a whuppin' on those girls. Seriously, kids know these kinds of things.

There's no riskier business than predicting a teenager's emotional swings, even for the brother or sister who shares a room and gets the inside info that Mom and Dad never hear. Losing by 50 or 150 points in a basketball game probably wasn't even the most important social event of the week. I'm guessing it had all the long-term emotional impact of a predance zit.

It's something you sort of remember years later and laugh at how little any of it meant. It builds character, right? Remember that saying? So if anyone needs postgame therapy, may I suggest it's not the Bloomington girls but their parents, along with the horrified callers to my show in the wake of the blowout. They might say their main interest is the continued emotional growth of their children, but they aren't comfortable traveling the road that ultimately achieves it.

# BETTER LATE THAN EVER

**I**'M HERE TO INFORM YOU that a tenet you've held dear your entire life is at best overrated and at worst an outright lie. Your parents preached it, and you've done your best to live it, but I'm going to give you the straight truth: punctuality isn't that big of a deal.

I'm speaking from personal experience, of course. Tardiness saved my career.

Several years ago, while I was working as a sports reporter for a local news channel in Portland, Oregon, I arrived late to a National Basketball Association shootaround. At the time, I still believed in the sanctity of punctuality, so I was a little frazzled and maybe even a bit sweaty. The first thing I saw was a group of reporters—roughly a dozen of them—chasing around an NBA journeyman who wasn't even trying to hide his contempt for every single one of them.

This guy was in trouble.

Again.

The pack, minus me, was hard on his heels.

Again.

It was my job to race over, grab a microphone, and join the beehive. Something important was happening—at least in the context of my life at the time—and it was incumbent upon me to make sure my station had the footage and the sound bite for six and eleven.

But I didn't do it. No, it was deeper than that: I *couldn't* do it. I stood and watched with a combination of amazement and disgust. I was paralyzed. It felt like I was watching my own funeral. I stood there, staring at the silliness of the swarm, and made the decision—right then and there—to change my entire professional career.

This wasn't an unusual scene. At the time, the Portland Trail Blazers were known as the Jail Blazers. They make every short list for most reprehensible group of humans who ever shared a locker room. But something about walking into this particular scene on this particular day bothered me more than it had before.

Maybe I was finally just fed up with covering a team whose roster was littered with guys who were better criminals than basketball players. Maybe the distance created by my lateness gave me a perspective that pushed me over the edge.

I stood, and I watched. The mob fumbled with pens and notebooks and cameras and microphones. Reporters jostled for position, elbowing one another. One tripped. They yelled questions to a man who was doing his best to pretend they didn't exist.

This entire Kabuki took place in the interest of one goal: to gain a sliver of access to a replaceable small forward with a penchant for collecting felonies and—beyond that—little or no interest in anything other than an orange ball.

I gave up on local television that day. I stayed in it for a while longer, but emotionally I had checked out. Radio was the answer. Radio would empower me to succeed on my own merit, to remove myself from the parasitic reporter-athlete relationship and stop chasing bad tips like a waiter at a cheap steakhouse.

I eventually joined the fray that day in Portland, halfheartedly and too late to experience the full force of the player's disdain.

It was one of the last times I dealt with a player solely on his terms.

*One* of the last times.

Several years after the Blazers had shed the "Jail" part, I was broadcasting my radio show from Los Angeles and was offered seats to a Lakers game by radio management. They asked me if I wouldn't mind popping my head into the locker room to make an appearance and let new Lakers like Steve Nash and Dwight Howard connect a face with my voice.

I walked in and looked around to see Howard, a six-foot-eleven all-star whose shoulders are so well defined it appears he has cantaloupes under his skin, wearing a towel and holding court with reporters.

He spotted me from across the room and stopped midsentence. He smiled, and in a voice that could be described only as gently threatening, said, "I hate you."

I wasn't the least bit offended. It didn't feel vicious, and I don't think it was intended that way. In fact, it drew a laugh from the people who were there.

Hey, it's part of the gig.

Green Bay's Aaron Rodgers, the most talented quarterback in the NFL, called me out in a live interview after he won the Super Bowl. "I'm glad my performance was up to your standards," he said. He was jabbing me because I'd spent the past several weeks questioning whether he deserved to be considered a superstar at such an early point in his career.

I laughed with Rodgers, too. At least I think he laughed. I know I did.

I've been through just about everything. The legendary Bobby Knight once knocked a microphone out of my hands. The late UNLV basketball coach Jerry Tarkanian once—or maybe it was twice—told me to fuck off. Chad Ochocinco Johnson—or whatever he's calling himself these days—once questioned my sex life on Twitter. Houston Texans running back Arian Foster took it a step further by questioning my humanity.

High-profile jocks and coaches routinely turn down invitations to appear on my show, and some of them do so by informing my diligent producers that they would rather swab the decks

of an oxygen-starved submarine than speak to me for five minutes on the air.

I don't wear any of this as a badge of honor. I don't consider
it a condemnation of my character, either. My job demands one
thing: I say what I see, and to hell with the fallout. My loyalty
isn't to my radio affiliates or sponsors or even fans. My loyalty is
to honesty—the truth as I see it. If I don't shoot straight, I'm no
good to anybody.

In the end, it's the only thing I've got. Wherever I go, it goes
with me. It's as loyal and unthreatening as a pet Labrador. If I
change jobs, it changes jobs, and its benefits never expire.

And you know what? Being loathed routinely and publicly
isn't all that different from what many other professionals face.
Lawyers sue and stonewall, politicians oppose and flip-flop,
principals fire and suspend, police officers pursue and arrest. Do
you think any of their adversaries greet them with flowers and
fist bumps after the decisions are made?

High-profile coaches in college and the NFL are insulated
from the real world not only by their wealth but also by the
public relations staff that shuttles them around and protects
them from any hint of serious questioning. The future
professional athletes are spotted and groomed early. From
before puberty, they're fawned over to the point of worship.
There is no dissent—sometimes not even any constructive
criticism—and definitely no scorn. So when they make it big,
the national media is often their first reality check. Predictably,
their skin is thin.

Look, every profession has its headaches. Mine just happens to be anger and resentment from rich and famous people. It's nothing I can't handle, but I often struggle to find a comparison that people will understand.

But I gave it some thought, and I think I nailed it: I have a lot in common with your friendly neighborhood IRS agent.

Although I'm guessing he's never late.

# HOW YOU REACT
## TO CRITICISM WILL
# ACTUALLY DEFINE
## HOW ACCURATE IT IS.

# WHEN EVERYONE'S A CRITIC, NO ONE'S A CRITIC

**I**T WAS THE MOST decorated film of 1991. To nearly every fan of the horror genre, it's a timeless classic. Despite public opinion, despite more than $272 million in box office gross, despite becoming the third movie ever to win Academy Awards for best film, best director, best actor, and best actress, *The Silence of the Lambs* was panned by respected critic Gene Siskel. The creepy serial killer, Buffalo Bill, played by actor Ted Levine, was not believable, he insisted. Even Siskel's television partner, the normally even-tempered Roger Ebert, was blown away by Siskel's opinion. So was I. More than two decades later, I can still remember the blue couch I was sitting on when Siskel delivered his shocking "thumbs-down."

With that kind of recall from more than twenty years ago, why is it that I can't remember what any movie critic said about any recent movie, even one from last month? Why is it that even the harshest political criticism now disappears quickly into the ether?

I have a hunch, and it goes like this: social media has changed the criticism game forever. Everyone is a member of the media now. The teenage girl on Facebook, the one who tells everyone how much she likes Katy Perry, is a media member. The angry troll on Twitter, the one who despises everything and everybody, is a media member. The amateur restaurant reviewer, the one who writes the granular two-thousand-word dissections on Yelp, is a media member.

If you have information that's newsworthy and the ability to disseminate it, you can voice an opinion that even the most powerful media might access, quote, and distribute. Your brand grows, and you don't even need qualifications. Sometimes it happens based on nothing more than titillation.

Along the way, though, criticism comes from so many people and so many angles and at such high velocity that it all congeals into a forgettable gelatin that spreads across our computer screens faster than we can wipe it off. And roughly eight minutes after we've cleared it, another wave hits. Remembering anything takes work.

The result is an empowered public and a whole generation of qualified critics whose opinions have been neutered. The average guest reviewer on Hotels.com may have as much power—at least in the eyes of the members of hotel management who read and react to it—as the movie or television or restaurant critic who has spent twenty years building his or her credibility.

This isn't great news for the average professional critic, probably, but it's occasionally turned into a gold mine for me.

My audience is now an army of unpaid employees. People across the country are willing and often capable correspondents; in the information business, then, the task falls to me. I have to simply root out the useless from the Pulitzer worthy, and I may have myself a good story or a smart theory without doing much of the legwork.

Dismiss the wisdom of the supposedly less-qualified public at your own risk. Arrogance kills the local grocer and the Wall Street hedge fund manager, and I'm not about to underestimate the power and reach of my listening audience. Let me give you just one example of a time when the public took the baton for the anchor leg of a 4x100 relay and finished the race for me.

Back in mid-January 2015, a bizarre story broke in which Australian PGA golfer Robert Allenby claimed he was beaten, robbed, and kidnapped in Honolulu at some point after leaving a wine bar after he'd missed the cut at the Sony Open. He posted photos on his Facebook page of his swollen, battered face, with a nasty, bloody scrape above his left eye. I closed my show on the Monday after the alleged incident by reading the report and saying, "This doesn't pass the smell test." I didn't make a big deal of it; in fact, I spent less than two minutes discussing Allenby's situation.

But then—*whoosh!*—the floodgates opened. Within thirty

minutes, I received emails from two PGA caddies and a top-twenty touring pro. When I arrived at work the next morning, I was greeted with a half dozen more emails, calls to my producer, and direct messages on Twitter from people connected with the PGA. I was able to validate that each one came from a legitimate source.

One missile after another was aimed directly at the Aussie.

"Don't buy Allenby's story," a caddie said. "He's not well liked. I'd never trust him."

A PGA pro said, "You're spot-on with your skepticism. Give this story another few days and watch what comes out."

He was right, except that it happened sooner than a few days. Two homeless people with nothing to gain—one reluctant even to share her story—told police that Allenby was so drunk he fell over and smashed his head on a lava rock in a park. The story began to melt away at the beginning of the week, and by Friday, it was nothing more than a puddle. Allenby never pressed charges, and the police, who didn't buy it from the beginning, never found the supposed assailants. It's understood within the golf community that the initial report—Allenby's report—was as wobbly as the golfer's legs on that fateful night.

I'm by no means saying the mainstream media should always rely on the public. I can also cite several dozen misses and fabrications that arrived yesterday alone. Those are generally easy to spot. Without going into specifics . . . well, if you must know, most of the time, the creative inventions are filled with regrettable grammar and a keyboard stuck on ALL CAPS.

We are definitely living in an uneasy time for reputable critics, but over the last decade, we've seen those without a voice gain one. We've seen those previously without leverage manage to acquire some. It's an equation that is universally applauded by the media when it's used to topple governments, but now they're finding that it can also intrude—and even squat—on their own real estate.

In Honolulu, two homeless people and a bunch of PGA people who reached out to me managed to derail the story of the millionaire golfer being beaten and kidnapped. Think about the convergence of those two groups. It could very well be the first time homeless people and professional golfers have worked in concert.

You might say it's par for the course these days.

# ODDS SQUAD

**Y**OU CAN TRY to persuade your kids to be more aggressive in youth sports with motivational speeches and dramatic reenactments of your own shattered dreams, but it becomes evident very early that aggressiveness is probably something that's more hardwired than acquired.

Maybe the little guy who dominates third-grade basketball has older brothers who rough him up. Maybe it's just the way he's always been. Whatever the case, it's probably not because his dad is prepping him for a run at a college scholarship.

Schools don't do boys any favors these days. Shortened recesses and cutbacks in physical education leave fewer places for them to burn their energy. That can be problematic in the classroom, but its impact is obvious on the field.

If you listen to parents watching their kids play an organized sport . . . first of all, I'm sorry. You and I hear the same chorus echoing from the bleachers. "Shoot it!" is generally followed by some form of "Don't let him do that!" It's plain to see that the kids who shoot, and the ones who actually do whatever it is that needs to be done—they're the same kids, of course—tend to carve up the other little dudes.

Many people are dissuaded by statistics that indicate your chances of winning the Powerball lottery are roughly 1 in 175 million. The odds of being in a plane crash are estimated to be 1 in 11 million, which is why most people don't have any qualms about jumping on a bird.

The odds of your son or daughter playing a professional sport are in that neighborhood, and yet the stands at a Little League game or a weekend hockey match are filled with parents who believe—and believe deeply, with every fiber of their being—that fewer turnovers will catapult their daughter to the WNBA, or that fewer strikeouts will eventually make their son the starting shortstop for the Baltimore Orioles.

It won't happen. And that's a very good thing.

Super Bowl XLIX between the New England Patriots and the Seattle Seahawks featured zero players who were five-star recruits coming out of high school. The Houston Texans' J. J. Watt, the most dominating defensive player in the league, didn't rate even a single solitary star. Aaron Rodgers played football at a junior college and was discovered only when coach Jeff Tedford of the UC Berkeley Golden Bears went to a game to recruit the team's tight end. Tom Brady and Joe Montana possessed such limited physical skills they dropped like rocks on draft day. You will currently find five or six really great quarterbacks roaming the face of the earth. Baseball scouts will tell you they don't think you can find a major league–caliber shortstop in the United States. Since LeBron James entered the NBA in 2003, the league has seen the emergence of maybe two transcendent talents, Blake Griffin and Anthony Davis. This country has not developed one soccer megastar.

And the path to get to these hallowed places, the college system, is increasingly a soul-sucking experience for an athlete. The college football season lasts about twenty-two weeks, and youth baseball—otherwise known as Ten Years a Parental Slave—begins at age twelve or younger. AAU (Amateur Athletic Union) basketball, the preferred one-stop shopping for top schools, is a gas-guzzling, weekend-surrendering obstacle course of caffeine (to keep you awake) and GPS (to find rural gyms). As for parents of hockey kids, do me a favor: open the checkbook, set the alarm clock, and be sure to check back with me in thirteen years.

With the odds the way they are, what's the expected payoff? If it's meant to provide fun, socialization, and physical activity, then good for you and your kid. Go for it. Keep it positive, healthy, and low-key, and you'll be enshrined in the Parent Hall of Fame. But I get the distinct impression, from a rapidly accumulating mountain of anecdotal evidence, including my own as a father of sons and daughters who play sports, that parental expectations are significantly higher than that. Many parents—*too many* parents—expect a literal payoff, in the form of a college scholarship or even a professional contract, from their investment in their children's sports career.

As I look at youth unemployment numbers and read the feedback from my shows, I wonder if those kids who are being pushed in sports would have been better served applying all that time and effort to something with a slightly higher success rate than one-tenth of 1 percent and a longer career than four and a half years, on average. Of course, the kids themselves didn't have much choice in the matter.

"Jump in the minivan, son, it's time for the endless trek to the lonely gym in the middle of somewhere for four hours of basketball. Dribbling is optional, passing prohibited."

I'm not saying it's wrong for kids to sample the experience. Organized sports can be an enriching activity. Your son is restless, and your daughter's friends are playing on the same soccer team, and it's not like kids these days are out playing baseball in vacant lots and basketball in the local park. You can't take your nine-year-old to many of the movies currently at the theater, and do you really want him home playing video games? It's either organized sports or obesity, in some cases.

But somewhere along the line, a shift occurred. The molecules changed, and it stopped being about the kid and started being about the parents. It's about *your* social life and *your* dreams. You watch football and know, deep down, that your kid isn't Megatron—or even Marginal-a-Tron—but you just can't help yourself.

Be prepared: after fifteen years of chasing a ball or a puck, your kids are going to be staring up at the kids whose parents looked at those daunting odds and decided to head in a different direction. Let's scale back a little on the sports thing, those parents thought, and maybe round out his life a bit.

I've watched the NCAA add games and practices to enrich something that has no relationship to the college experience. I've seen football players, even at the traditional powers, leave their programs mentally burned out and physically torn up. They've been funneled through easy classes that fit into a schedule that includes four hours of football a day, so they're not even reaping the academic rewards of being on campus.

But the coach? Oh, the coach made out just fine. He's got a monstrous new contract, an endorsement deal with the local Mercedes dealer, and a sweet house on the lake. Meanwhile, that burned-out running back—by the way, there are now seven on the roster—never did fulfill his dream of starting just one college game.

The travel schedules for college sports such as soccer, basketball, and baseball are so daunting it's hard to understand how they're even allowed. Basketball teams drop kids into hotels at three in the morning to catch a few hours of sleep before a televised game that night. After four years of that, you know your way around a Holiday Inn Express breakfast buffet but next to nothing about a profession. Yes, there are some, like my friend Doug Gottlieb, a basketball star at Oklahoma State in the early 1990s and now a respected sportscaster, who contends that college sports gave him a life he wouldn't have otherwise. He's not alone in that belief, and maybe I'm being too cynical.

But go stare at those success-rate numbers and try to square them with the hours devoted to trying to beat them. Look at the wear and tear on those young bodies. Think of your corporate hours and add 30 percent. That's the "dream" you're pursuing: a four-year grind that sends them down an assembly line and turns them into another forgettable serial number in the sports lug-nut factory.

Tonight, on a cable network near you.

Here's something I guarantee you won't realize at the time it happens: when your son or daughter comes home in tears after being cut or relegated to the bench, use that night for a little family reevaluation. It's not the darkest hour or the saddest moment.

Don't consider it the death of a dream. Consider it the birth of reality.

If you play it right, your child will not only go to college but also actually be a college student. That sad night, with all the tears and angst and end-of-the-world drama, could be the best day of their lives, and yours.

PEOPLE WHO REFUSE TO
TAKE "NO" FOR AN
ANSWER USUALLY
DON'T HEAR "NO"
MUCH FOR AN
ANSWER.

# RAY OF LIGHT

**T**HERE'S NO QUESTION A GAP—no, a chasm—exists between the way professional athletes and fans think on many issues, and there's no greater example than the relationship that legendary NFL linebacker Ray Lewis has with both groups.

Lewis is a fascinating study. Built something like a tree stump with an easy, contagious laugh, Lewis is difficult to dislike in person. If you happen to show a little uneasiness or awe around him, he has a disarming ability to make you feel comfortable. The first time he and I met, years ago, we talked about football like we had known each other since childhood. His sheer passion made him both intimidating and vulnerable.

Years after that first meeting, after I had just finished a radio show in Scottsdale, Arizona, during Super Bowl week in 2015, I found myself attempting to navigate a sea of fans on my way to a scheduled event. I was in desperate need of a distraction if I was going to get to the waiting SUV in time. Over the years, I've learned to rely on the oldest trick in the book: if you're an athlete or media person looking to avoid being besieged with requests for selfies and autographs, you wait for a person with a bigger name to emerge and then quickly duck behind him. In other words, use fame as a shield to get where you need to be.

And at precisely my moment of greatest need, as luck would have it, I spotted Lewis leaving the *SportsCenter* set after an appearance.

I looked into the sea of hungry fans and yelled, "Hey, look! The greatest linebacker ever—Ray Lewis!" Lewis, whose back was toward me, turned around, saw me, and immediately broke into a laugh. It's a trick he'd undoubtedly seen dozens of times. For the next minute or so, Lewis signed footballs and pennants. When he was pushed ahead by ESPN security to get him on his way, a handful of male fans started taking some verbal shots at him. These, of course, were the same fans who would sell Lewis's signature on eBay or brag about it for weeks.

Everybody who follows sports knows the source of this vitriol: On January 31, 2000, early on Monday morning after the Rams beat the Titans in the Super Bowl in Atlanta, two young men were shot and killed. Lewis originally was charged with two counts of murder but pleaded down to obstruction of justice in exchange for testifying against two of his companions that night. Neither one was convicted, but the stain of that night will cling to Lewis forever. Few people know what happened that night. Even fewer probably know what happened with Kobe Bryant on July 1, 2003, in Colorado, where he was charged with—and later acquitted of—sexual assault against a nineteen-year-old hotel employee. And it could be that only Bobby Knight and his hunting buddy know what happened that day in October of 1999, when Knight shot his friend—accidentally, Knight says—on a hunting trip. That's the thing about many of these enduring, defining moments: you don't really know.

A few nights after I pulled my dodge-and-duck on Lewis in Scottsdale, the topic arose during a dinner with a notable NFL player. Over several bottles of cabernet, this player shared his admiration for Lewis and talked about their friendship. He grew more passionate as the conversation lengthened, and tears formed in his eyes when he told me that Lewis was one of only three people he would die for. Several nights later, this time with Bill Romanowski, another polarizing ex-linebacker, Lewis's name came up again. Romo spoke of him not only with admiration but also outright reverence.

Not every player admires Lewis. Not every player admires retired quarterbacks Troy Aikman or Brett Favre, either. But Lewis occupies a unique space among players. He is viewed as giving, which few players are. He is viewed as loyal, a quality that many promise but far fewer deliver. I heard repeated stories of him reaching out in crises and asking nothing in return—a truly rare trait in a world of selfish alpha males perpetually seeking to elevate their brands. Mention his name among players, and they smile and share a story. There's almost never an exception.

Among fans outside of Baltimore, it's a far different story. To them, Lewis is a treacherous, intimidating man. He's the perfect storm of trouble, from that night in Atlanta, to his swagger as a college star with the Miami Hurricanes, to that night in Atlanta, to his pregame preening in the NFL, to—you got it—that night in Atlanta.

Courts decide events such as the one that took place on the street in Atlanta. But when you speak with people who have worked with or alongside Lewis, his reputation becomes more nuanced. Shades of gray appear everywhere. People speak of a refinement that doesn't fit the prevailing narrative. If it's an act, it's Brando-esque. If it's a con, it's Enron.

What if the best person you ever met had done the most horrible thing? What if your most trusted friend had once been deceptive? What if the woman with whom you had shared your deepest trust had once sold it out?

Ray Lewis, like most of us, is a complex man. I don't envy his life or admonish it. He is a human flashpoint, though, and everyone has something to say about him.

The fans say one thing.

The players say another.

I don't have the answers, and neither do you.

Whose word do you trust? What actions do you believe?

# STRAIGHT, NO CHASER

**B**ACK IN THE DAYS when Mike Tyson's left hook was destroying the world, sports journalists didn't cover him so much as follow him. And by *follow*, I don't mean the way a baseball beat writer covers a team, I mean *follow* as in *track*, and sometimes even *chase*.

Covering Iron Mike as a young sportscaster required several attributes, chief among them patience. Nobody canceled or changed more workouts. Nobody had a more unreliable or less informative posse than the champ. Nobody cared less about appeasing the reporters assigned to follow him.

Tyson never spoke before workouts, and his sycophantic entourage, which disdained everything but pretty girls and whatever gifts someone might be willing to provide for them, only amplified his legendary moodiness.

But Tyson never promised anything, neither access nor charm nor even the occasional acknowledgment that he knew you were alive. And so the days that I was assigned to follow him became miniadventures. I put on a different hat, happy to break the monotony of sitting half-attentively as some coaching dullard spouted clichés from a dais. Tyson was different; he was *alive*. He was that dark alley that kept you on your toes and, in the end, made you a more perceptive and creative reporter.

And over the course of my time in Las Vegas, I came to appreciate the biggest pain in the ass I ever covered.

In a similar fashion, Dennis Rodman didn't endorse fresh salads and deliver cheeseburgers to the pressroom. Neither did megalomaniacal NFL wide receiver Terrell Owens. Famed NBA enigma Allen Iverson mocked practice. Young quarterback Johnny Manziel of the Cleveland Browns, who spent part of his first NFL offseason in a rehab facility, is practically a walking sandwich board that hawks entitlement on both sides. Yet on we go, blissfully ignoring the blaring lights and warning sirens.

The sports world is full of subtle dysfunction, passive-aggressive locker-room destroyers, and agents hired to hide their clients' worst traits. Amid that backdrop, couldn't I make the argument that those players we most often ridicule—the sullen and the mean, the outlandish and the irascible—are also the most honest?

If you want an authentic glimpse into the money-soaked, fame-obsessed, ultracompetitive world of sports, the best guide is a coach or athlete willing to show his chaotic, messy side.

Rodman, Ochocinco, Manziel, the mercurial former Portland TrailBlazer J. R. Rider—they all wear their 'tudes on their lapels.

The general managers who signed Rodman were no different from the pharmaceutical salesman who dates the Dallas stripper and expects her to become a dutiful housewife and life-long caregiver. Dude, when you met her in February, she was allowing long-haul truckers to jam singles into her G-string inside a building with no windows. And by summer you expected what? A character from a Nora Ephron script? The Barefoot Contessa?

Save your anger for the deceptive, not the dysfunctional. Mock the manipulative, not the mischievous.

Jim Harbaugh had a winning percentage of almost 70 percent when the San Francisco 49ers canned him in 2015 after four seasons as head coach. Consider coaching legends such as Bill Parcells, Chuck Noll, and Marv Levy: their winning percentages all hovered around 56 percent, albeit over many more seasons.

Did Harbaugh lose his job because he was gruff and intense, or did he get whacked because general manager Trent Baalke expected Harbaugh to be someone different from the guy he originally hired? Because if there's one thing you can say with certainty about Harbaugh, it's this: his personality has never been a secret. Several coaches who either worked with or competed against Harbaugh told me of his bug-eyed, borderline-scary intensity—and I didn't even have to ask. It was a matter of record that Harbaugh was a walking migraine during his years at Stanford University except for those three or four hours he spent on the sideline every fall Saturday.

When Lance Stephenson bolted the Indiana Pacers for the Charlotte Hornets in 2014, rumors began to swirl. My goodness, he might not be an ideal fit for a young, rebuilding club. Really? Did Hornets executives miss the part where he was arrested for allegedly pushing his girlfriend down the stairs in 2010? Did they miss the 2014 Eastern Conference Finals, when Stephenson blew into LeBron James's ear *during play?* Did the South experience a widespread power outage that night?

It's not my mission to empower or excuse the malcontents, but I wouldn't mind exploring the reasons why we fail to comprehend their decidedly unmixed messages.

Sports provides certain flashpoints that ignite young people with combustible personalities. Elements like sudden wealth, instant notoriety, and plenty of free time can upend even the most stable people. Mix those ingredients with a twentysomething who doesn't have the background to handle it, and you get a powder keg in a pair of size-17 Nikes.

A pattern develops. Just for curiosity's sake, was it the first or the second time Alex Rodriguez lied publicly about performance-enhancing drugs that raised New York Yankees general manager Brian Cashman's suspicions?

Shouldn't we subject the executives, coaches, and scouts who miss—or, worse, ignore—obvious warning signs to a higher level of scorn than we do the athlete who just got out of his teenage years?

Shame on the woman who dates the bad boy and then complains that he fights and flirts. He wore his brand—and his brawn—on his sleeve.

Tyson would occasionally train at the cramped and historic Johnny Tocco's Ringside Gym. This was before he became a national tragedy and treasure (tragic national treasure?). The late owner of the gym was a gentler version of Burgess Meredith's crusty Mickey Goldmill character in the first three *Rocky* movies, and he once summed up boxing's most maddening and enigmatic figure in two simple sentences:

"I don't have any problem with Tyson," said Tocco. "He pays his bills, and I don't expect anything from him that he can't handle."

# 5-HOUR ENERGY

HAS MADE A DECAF VERSION,

## FOR THE CONSUMER

INTERESTED IN JUST THE

# RANCID TASTE.

# THE FIX IS IN

**P**ETER LOTTERHOS GREW UP in a house with two psycho-
therapists as parents, so it's no coincidence he ended up
choosing life coaching and therapy as a profession. More than
fifteen years of sitting around that dinner table, talk of the
human psyche ping-ponging back and forth, probably made it
inevitable.

I have a confession to make: I lack the patience for a
weekend-long seminar, and I definitely lack both the patience
and the interest to sit and listen to other people recount their
life histories for hours on end. And so, with my personality faults
on the table, I wrote Peter a big check and told him to come
over on a Saturday for an intensive one-on-one mental workout.
We had met several times before, but I needed a good cry, so I
decided what the hell—let's take a trip back to my childhood to

unpack some of the remaining baggage so that we can head out and hit a few golf balls afterward.

Peter taped a large white sheet to the wall and proceeded to use a blue marker to retrace my childhood: all the memories and conflicts and confusion we carry around like dumbbells. Five exhausting hours later, we'd put some of my baggage on a one-way flight to nowhere, hoping it never returns.

First, therapy teaches me that most of our fears are exaggerated. All of that childhood drama starts as a tiny kernel in our brains and grows until the embellishment can no longer fit into the tiny space provided. It's fascinating how a small event can be instrumental in creating insecurities and doubts well into adulthood.

Second, therapy forces—for me, anyway—a paradigm shift. It allows you to start focusing your energy in the right direction. Problems start getting solved instead of extended.

I always think that Major League Baseball could use counseling's second result every time it starts to discuss shortening games in order to increase its appeal to younger fans.

Sit down for a minute, seamheads, and let's ferret out the game's real problems. For one thing, college football games now last twenty-five minutes longer than they did a decade ago, and the television ratings are up sharply. The NFL numbers—TV ratings, revenue, fan interest—continue to grow even though pro games last even longer than college games. Hurry-up offenses actually lengthen games: more incompletions, more clock stoppages. And yet the no-huddle has added to the interest in college football, and it has crept its way into the NFL, most notably with the Chip Kelly–led Philadelphia Eagles. Its appeal is obvious: it adds more actual activity.

And now we pause to reflect on baseball's real problem. In fact, let me grab the big blue marker, walk to the big white sheet on the wall, and spell it out in large letters:

## MORE ACTION NEEDED!

Guess what? Lower the mound and shrink the strike zone, and suddenly averages will rise. In no time, you'll find that pitchers will nibble less and throw more strikes. Even if it means more walks, that's okay. You know why? Because it will create more base runners, which will create more stolen bases and more guys running from first to third and second to home, which will create more close plays on the base paths. In other words, and say it out loud along with me:

More athletes—*lots* more of them—running around doing athletic things on a baseball field.

Yes, we have shorter attention spans. Making sure, as baseball did before the 2015 season, that batters keep a foot in the batter's box could shave a good ten to twelve minutes from games, but who complains about time when they're watching an action-packed sport? From concerts, to airline flights, to dates, to car rides with your kids, visual stimuli make time less relevant. Do you really think a 3:04 game reduced to 2:51 is a game changer? After eleven minutes of opera, I'm out. But if that soprano were juggling, I'm guessing I'd last until the first intermission.

With human growth hormone, amphetamines, and steroids out of the sport (presumably), hitters are tired. They play every day, unlike pitchers, and the constant grind results in a distinct loss of power. The 2014 World Series had more than one hundred hits, and only five were home runs. Even more discouraging, more than 72 percent were singles. And those were the lucky ones who managed to get on base despite a strike zone roughly the size of a Times Square video board. Over the span of the sport's rich history, rules have been altered more than twenty times in an attempt to help offenses. There's a reason for that: it keeps us more interested.

And speaking of tired, as you can see, I'm heading back toward the sheet with the blue marker in my hand. I'm going to spell out baseball's second deep, troubling childhood issue, this time in even bigger block letters:

## FEWER GAMES, PLEASE!

Oh, I know all the reasons why this isn't realistic (money), but for the love of ultramarathoning, can we scale back the season from an insane amount of games to—I don't know—maybe an *absurd* amount? The length of the baseball season—one hundred and sixty-two regular-season games, plus six weeks of spring training, plus a month of postseason—makes presidential campaigns feel like an Olympic hundred-meter final. Research shows that fans, more than ever, need to feel urgency in the sports they watch. People are busier, their options more voluminous, so unless there's a sense that they absolutely *must* watch, fans won't—at least not at the national level. Local ratings remain excellent, though, so the folks in Boston, San Francisco, and Detroit don't want fewer games. And let's face it: there's a level of resignation at work here, too. Blazing summer humidity in much of the country forces many of us indoors, and baseball is about the only live event we've got.

It's no wonder that hitters are overmatched. The strike zone is the size of a tarmac. Nearly every young pitcher is running it up there in the midnineties. Staffs are deeper, which makes for more pitching changes. If you've got a bat in your hands, you're entitled to have a clinical-level persecution complex.

So lower that mound and shrink the zone, baseball. There's a reason flying from New York to LA seems faster now, and it's not an accelerated jet stream. It's the television set and the Wi-Fi on board to occupy your mind.

The task at hand isn't so much about keeping it short. It's about making what you've got more compelling.

And in the interest of improved mental health, allow me to put that in big blue letters.

# A MISTAKE UNKNOWN
# TO MANKIND

**T**ALK RADIO OPERATES in its own weird sub-universe. The primary goal is to achieve greatness, but if you can't deliver on that, terrible isn't a bad second option. Be great. Be awful. Everything in between is just white noise, rarely heard and always forgotten. No other business would ever operate like this.

*Man, you've got to stay at the Marriott next time you're in Philadelphia. They screwed up everything, and it was awesome.*

Terrible—often more than great—garners attention in radio. With all the entertainment options available to the consumer, an awkward or downright disastrous segment can translate into digital download gold. As a host, the difference is one of control: you can plan to create greatness, but catastrophic just sort of happens on its own. It unfolds without warning, on its own time, and you end up with a hot, smoldering mess all over yourself.

On July 1, 2015, I was the one trying to clean up after Michigan football coach Jim Harbaugh made an appearance on my show. I knew all about his legendary rigidity, so I wasn't expecting him to show up as Winston Churchill. I anticipated nothing resembling a verbal masterpiece, but I thought his quirkiness and marquee value would prove captivating for a few minutes.

Instead, I gradually sank into radio quicksand.

The more I prodded, the more he stammered. The more I poked, the more he hesitated. The more I said, the less he understood. How bad was it? We had a lengthy and mostly inarticulate back and forth about the difference between "bye" and "buy." It became the Joe DiMaggio's 56-game hitting streak of "I don't knows" over the course of six minutes. It's a record that'll never be broken.

And maybe Harbaugh really *didn't* know, but I definitely did. It was painful. Even *my* joints hurt listening to us.

Did the questions piss him off or was he just not in the mood to talk? Either way, I couldn't stick around to find out. I mercifully ended the clunkiest and oddest interview of my career, took a deep breath, and tried to regain some semblance of talk-show momentum.

Whether or not Harbaugh will be back on any show of mine is irrelevant—what I do know is that he will be deeply missed by the San Francisco 49ers. I feel so strongly about this prediction that it's my NFL lock of the next decade. Coming to an interstate near you: the Niners, minus my friend Jimbo, will be a smoldering, traffic-snarling tire fire for years.

The 49ers will not win a division title over the next ten years.

They will watch Seattle Seahawks quarterback Russell Wilson dissect them until his final years, and then they will watch his replacement do the same thing.

If you need to place blame, lay it at the feet of silver-spooned owner Jed York, who parlayed his family lineage—his uncle is former owner Eddie DeBartolo, his father is former owner John York—into the dual role of owner and CEO at twenty-seven years of age. The Bay Area sports media have already figured out what the rest of the country will eventually come to recognize: over the next ten years, York will be the poster boy for how *not* to run an NFL team, and for how taking something important for granted is the worst move of all.

First, let's speak to an undeniable truth of the game: even if you do everything well as a coach—assess talent astutely, develop players quickly, manage the game and the clock brilliantly—you will struggle to win 60 percent of your games. It's a cruel game, especially at the professional level, mostly because drafting the right players is really an educated guess. College players can look great on tape and while working out in their underwear for a week at the NFL scouting combine, but do they have the stomach for NFL-level contact and the pressures that come with performing as a professional?

Winning is hard if you do things right, impossible if you do them poorly. Yes, you can land a superstar quarterback to make your life easier, but even that's no guarantee. Peyton Manning landed in head coach John Fox's lap in Denver, and Fox still got canned in 2015 for underachieving.

What York and 49ers management want you to believe is that Jim Harbaugh's accomplishments could have been achieved by any number of people. They believe that he fell into the fortunate position of being able to benefit from the all-knowing, all-seeing genius of York and general manager Trent Baalke. Harbaugh, they whisper, sort of got in the way. He actually blew the chance for their magnificent roster to win several Super Bowls.

That was the only take anyone could have had after reading the scorching assessment of Harbaugh from anonymous sources in Seth Wickersham's 2014 story on the coach in *ESPN the Magazine*. After reading it, you were left wondering whether Harbaugh could manage to perform everyday functions like putting eggs in a grocery cart without first breaking them over his head. The quotes were so personal, detailed, and slanted that they could have come only from a boss with an ax to grind. This is what happens in pro sports when alpha males fight to obtain power and get credit. First, they start to believe their own press clippings, and then they take the next step: use them to wound others.

In the land of deluded football fantasies, they believe Harbaugh is the luckiest of all the lucky souls. In reality, though, he walked into a smoking mess of a franchise that hadn't won ten games in a season in a decade, was 5-11 the previous year, 2010, and was led by the physically and mentally battered Alex Smith. In Harbaugh's first season, the 49ers went 13-3.

How lucky was Harbaugh? So lucky that he could go to the NFC Championship game with Smith at quarterback. Smith is a good guy, but his lack of arm strength limits the scope of any offense he runs. Smith was later traded to Kansas City, and, even working under the clever offensive mind of head coach Andy Reid in an era of pass-happy football, Smith did the impossible in 2015: he went an entire season without throwing a touchdown pass to a wide receiver.

If the engineers at the Oracle Corporation, just up the road from the 49ers' stadium, examined every statistic in NFL history, they'd have a hard time finding a more unlikely outcome. Seriously, those are some Powerball odds.

Harbaugh didn't stop winning after that first season in San Francisco. He followed it with two more trips to the NFC Championship game and a Super Bowl. He was one "lucky" dude whose true colors were apparent only during a disappointing and injury-riddled 8-8 season in his final year as coach.

As a tiny aside—and I sincerely hope this doesn't get in the way of documenting Harbaugh's incompetence—he had previously coached at two nonfootball schools, the University of San Diego and Stanford, and won big at both. As a matter of fact, Stanford was a bigger shipwreck than San Francisco, and yet he lucked his way into building that program into a perennial Bowl Championship Series team.

Perhaps an even clearer sign that Harbaugh maybe-sorta-kinda knew what he was doing transpired after York whacked him in January 2015. He went to take over the University of Michigan Wolverines, and several of his top assistants left with him. A few months later, dependable running back Frank Gore signed with the Indianapolis Colts, where he stands a better chance of proving he's not an old horse ready for the glue factory. Shortly afterward, Patrick Willis, a tremendous linebacker from his first day in the league, suddenly and shockingly retired at the age of thirty. A week after that, twenty-four-year-old rookie revelation Chris Borland, who'd replaced the injured Willis, quit football because of his concerns about football's connection to chronic brain trauma.

How could this be? The franchise had just promoted defensive line coach Jim Tomsula, and York praised him as being beloved by the players. And yet top players and coaches were suddenly bolting?

As I write this, in late March 2015, I know that I will watch Tomsula's 49ers and Harbaugh's Wolverines without an ounce of anxiety or uncertainty. I know exactly what will happen: Michigan will gradually turn into a proud and winning program; Tomsula's team will be competitive, playing with the energy that people manage to find when performing for new bosses, but eventually it will lack the leadership needed to win with any sort of consistency. The 49ers will plummet in their division, buried beneath Seattle and Arizona.

I would bet each and every one of you individually if you were interested. I would bet everything short of my family if I could. Hey, a man has to believe passionately in something, right?

And I finalize my thoughts by borrowing a line from the most intense and passionate football coach in the game today:

I will watch this happen with the kind of passion unknown to mankind.

I'VE GONE TO THERAPY.
I'M STILL A MESS!
FIND MY INNER SELF? I DID.
I HATED HIM!

# BUGSY'S LAST MEAL

Our FRENCH BULLDOG, BUGSY, was nearing the end after fourteen years, and my wife, Ann, decided on a last meal of chicken parmigiana and a dark chocolate bar. Dogs aren't supposed to eat chocolate, but humans aren't supposed to ingest or inhale drugs, either, and we all know the reality behind that. Bugsy devoured both the entrée and the dessert and smiled. French bulldogs do that.

My wife watched him the whole time and said he was in pre-heaven.

For the first forty-nine years of my life, I didn't understand it when families mourned over pets as if they were family members. My first family dog was Corky, and my late mother said he followed me wherever I roamed around our home in a coastal Washington state exurb. Corky was like a four-legged GPS, allowing my mom to know my exact location in the dunes just beyond our neighborhood. When he passed away, I just figured we could always get another dog. It might take a few days. You can't do that with people.

The morning after Bugsy had his last meal, we took him as a family to the vet and gave him one last hug. We brought his bed to make it more comfortable for him, saving him the indignity of the cold metal table, and my wife said she could feel his spirit leaving his little body as she bawled and the kids started hugging one another.

Someone once said that the older you get, the dumber you realize you are. With any luck and some curiosity, your life broadens, and you realize there are so many things you don't really understand. You think back on so many moments when you lacked empathy or understanding, and all you want to do is call everyone you ever offended.

For forty-nine years, I questioned all those people who cried over the death of a dog. I mocked them on the radio and shook my head at their silliness. Then Bugsy died, and I gained focus as my vision blurred from tears.

That sounds corny, I know, but so did a funeral for a pet.

Until your family lives through one.

Life is like that.

# ROOT CAUSE

**T**HE DRIVE WAS LONG AND LONELY: three days through four states, and my only company was my 1984 AMC Pacer and its Blaupunkt AM radio.

It started in tiny Anacortes, Washington, where I spent the weekend with my college girlfriend before packing the Pacer with all my possessions and heading for Las Vegas to begin a career in broadcasting. I received my first speeding ticket in Eureka, California, and in Sacramento I drove through a massive cloudburst for the first and only time. The rain and hail were so intense that every vehicle came to a virtual standstill on a busy freeway. On to Fresno, where I was confronted and nearly robbed in the laundry room of a cheap hotel, and southeast to Nevada, where the Pacer overheated minutes after crossing the state line.

All of those moments were memorable, in the way that new and uncertain adventures always are, but they were mere appetizers in comparison to the meal—both literal and metaphorical—that remains embedded in my mind to this day.

As I headed into the last few hours of the trip, after the laundry room experience and before the overheated car, I pulled into a combination restaurant–gas station for a quick bite and some gasoline. It's probably not true, but Baker, California, felt to me like the most desolate place within our fifty states where a lonely traveler could find both gas and food.

Baker is surrounded by death—it's on the southern tip of Death Valley, at the intersection of Interstate 15 and Death Valley Road—and it looks and feels like no other place in the world. No vegetation, no pulse.

Under the usual searing sun, I sat on a bench inhaling lunch. I looked up at one point and noticed a little girl to the side of the restaurant, alone, playing in the dirt with a small, dirty toy. Her manner indicated to me that she was both comfortable and accustomed to this practice, and when she stood up and walked through a side door into the restaurant, my suspicions were confirmed: this was her parents' restaurant, and this was her home. She had spent her life to that point in the desert, in a town that felt to me like Mars with a truck stop, and she had spent most of it by herself, with only a small toy for amusement.

That little girl has shaped an ideology that I repeat so often it annoys even my most ardent fans. I repeat it weekly:

"Evolve and grow or die. If not for you, then for the little people whose lives you control."

It seemed to me, a guy straight out of college excited to start a new chapter in my life, that the little girl was born with no chance. I might be wrong. Maybe she went on to a rich life of red carpets and intellectual advancement, but it sure didn't feel like she was headed for that path. The way it played out in my mind, she was born into a lifeless community with few friends and fewer opportunities, forced to while away her days in the dirt. Her busy parents, intent on paying the next round of bills, had no choice but to allow her to to amuse herself for large parts of the day.

A lucky few are born on third base, but most of us begin our lives somewhere near first, either leading off or heading for the bag. But what about the kid who is so removed from the field that she finds herself locked in the laundry room behind the clubhouse? Maybe it wasn't precisely true in the case of the little girl, but it certainly is for millions of other kids.

Do any of us truly realize how much our lives are dramatically altered, for better or worse, based on our parents' dreams, capabilities, and limitations? Do we understand that a child's potential can be squandered, or never materialize in the first place, simply because of geography or family? Do we understand how inherently random all of this can be?

Forty percent of Americans will never move more than twenty miles from their hometowns, which is fine, I guess, unless you have kids.

When we argue about social programs that aim to help the poorest among us, are we discussing an issue of political ideology or human potential? Shouldn't politics serve as a pretext for the bigger and largely untapped reason to lend a hand? Many of our greatest performers, from engineering to the arts, come from backgrounds that can be considered disadvantaged. Once they are given a shot, though, they elevate not only their own lives but ours as well.

I travel mostly by airplane now, but whenever I drive between Las Vegas and Los Angeles, I always stop in Baker. There's a Greek café that has wonderful gyros, but that bench and that restaurant are gone, or maybe just replaced.

That little girl is probably in her thirties now. Maybe she's happier and healthier than the rest of us. Maybe she rose up from that patch of dirt to create life that enriches all of us in some way. It would be nice to think that way, and it sure feels better, but it ignores the statistical near certainty that she's not.

# ATHLETES WITH "I CAN'T BREATHE" T-SHIRTS AREN'T TELLING YOU WHAT TO THINK. THEY'RE TELLING YOU WHAT *THEY* THINK.

# POLISHED FOR YOUR PROTECTION

**Y**OU KNOW THE TYPE of bar that's hot at the moment but clearly destined to close within a year? You know how you can feel it when you're there—that it's fun and happening, but you know everyone there will migrate to some newer and hotter place within weeks? Well, this time it was in Tampa, and on this particular night I learned a valuable lesson about honesty. It can be distilled down to this: people like honesty only when they agree with it. When they don't, honesty changes into something else entirely, like crassness or meanness or idiocy.

The genesis of my discovery was hardly earth-shattering. Rich McKay, who was then the general manager of the Tampa Bay Buccaneers, told me privately in a television studio that Danny Wuerffel—local fan favorite, star at the University of Florida, 1996 Heisman Trophy winner—was not an NFL-caliber quarterback. His arm wasn't strong enough, an assessment that would become obvious during his brief professional career. Publicly, though, McKay said wonderful, glowing things about Wuerffel's work ethic and character, the football equivalent of "She's got a nice personality."

That night in the bar, though, McKay's opinion carried zero weight. A conversation with a fan grew heated when I had the audacity to inform him that his favorite quarterback's NFL career would be short-lived.

Hey—he asked; I told.

This fan wanted a certain answer—the answer that backed what he believed. When he got something else, he showed that he lacked the basic coping mechanisms possessed by most people with above-motor-oil-grade IQs.

It initially confounded me. Don't people want the real skinny? Don't fans want the inside dirt—the behind-the-scenes, unvarnished reality—rather than the spit-shined PR release that follows? Who wants antiseptic over authentic?

Most fans, actually. They want to feel good about their heroes, especially the ones who represent their city or town.

Unfortunately, this phenomenon is the background music of my career. I gather information from sources, directly and indirectly, to feed my radio and television shows. The information often reflects poorly on specific teams, coaches, and franchises, and I pass it along to fans who are ravenous for insight—as long as it's optimistic and wrapped with a shiny bow.

Do longtime Indiana Hoosiers basketball fans, those who

still worship the tempestuous Bobby Knight, want to know that he often treated ESPN employees with the same disdain normally reserved for Big Ten referees and his least favorite players? Do they want to know that he did so little homework before going on the air that even his most ardent backers were discouraged?

Nah. Most don't.

Chicago Cubs fans fumed in 2002 when sportswriter Rick Reilly pressed slugger Sammy Sosa, a man strongly suspected but not proven of taking performance-enhancing drugs, to give a urine sample before a game, even though Sosa had challenged the media to do just that. Reilly was one of many informed reporters who knew that Sosa was baseball's biggest phony. He projected a wholesome image to the public, sure, but one former big leaguer who played against him told me, "He's a dog. He presents one thing and lives another." When I mentioned Sosa's habit of broadcasting his Catholic faith by ostentatiously making the sign of the cross before every at bat, the player just laughed and rolled his eyes. Enough said.

Until Sosa's career in Chicago crumbled amid infighting and petty jealousies, that story would have been met with outrage.

Two top football coaches told me that the head-coaching position at the University of Texas is the most overrated job in sports. How would that go over with Longhorns fans? And not only that, but they told me that coaches love to have their name associated with the job in Austin for one reason: it gives them leverage to get a raise at their current jobs. They say the neediness of the powerful Longhorns boosters, the layers of bureaucracy to navigate, and the number of Texas-sized egos and asses that demand to be kissed means the job comes with an endless conveyor belt of distractions.

Yeah, that wouldn't sit well with the Longhorns faithful.

After twenty-five years in this industry, I've accumulated dozens of contacts. In my world, they're called sources. They're more than willing to talk, and each one has his or her own reason. Some want to elevate their case or push a narrative. Others are simply straight shooters who have grown tired of the hypocrisy being peddled to the public. Fully aware of the reach of my audience, these guys talk and talk and then keep on talking.

My cell phone contact list is filled with sports personalities, which means that my head is filled with hilarious and unflattering stories.

But that night in Tampa taught me a little something about the value of those stories: when in public, confronted face-to-face by preconceived ideas, giving people exactly what they want to hear ensures a safer and far less hostile environment. Sometimes honesty can wait.

# SAW SOMETHING, SAID SOMETHING

THERE'S NO POLITICALLY CORRECT WAY of saying this: fit, in his twenties, and poking his head out of his hotel door to look up and down the narrow hotel hallway, the young man looked deeply suspicious. I walked out of the elevator seconds earlier to see a security guard whispering into his walkie-talkie. Clearly, this man—prime age for committing crime—was trouble in a dark T-shirt.

It was Super Bowl week, the perfect time for a publicity-seeking troublemaker, and just about every possibility raced through my head as I made two quick lefts and began the tense forty-yard walk past his door on the way to my room.

I tried to look cool and no doubt failed. I never made eye contact as I passed him and headed for my suite in a New Orleans hotel. Something in my head told me that any attention

I paid him would only make matters worse, but I was on heightened alert as I quickened my pace past his door. I could hear noise mixed with confusion and what sounded a lot like anger coming from inside his room. Banking hard around a corner, I quickly unlocked my door and immediately dialed the hotel operator. As the commercial says, "If you see something, say something." This, I was sure, was *something*.

The polite lady in guest services informed me the man was actually a college kid who was running late to a wedding. He was nervously waiting for a second suitcase, and the security officer on the floor was communicating with the bell captain to ensure a successful delivery.

Clearly, the story I concocted in my head was far more sinister.

*Creepy* is a concept that's hard to decipher and even harder to explain. It can be confused with awkwardness or anxiety—the kid peeking out the door is proof of that—but that doesn't mean your first instincts are always incorrect.

Take an incident that took place three years ago, when we were about to tape a segment on *SportsNation*, an ESPN show I formerly cohosted. As we made last-minute arrangements for the show, star Minnesota Vikings running back Adrian Peterson was being introduced to members of the staff. This was a scene that had played out countless times with dozens of pro athletes or coaches, and they were all—almost to a man—fast and forgettable meetings. They're a perfunctory part of the job, and even the most memorable moments were innocuous. I remember 49ers head coach Jim Harbaugh being more bored than most, and I remember mixed martial arts fighter Jon "Bones" Jones being surprisingly witty. I walked away from a meeting with another NFL running back, Arian Foster, thinking he had a lucrative postfootball career in television if he wanted it.

The five minutes we spent with Peterson were different, landing somewhere near—and maybe even beyond—the line separating uncomfortable and distressing. Appearing to be chiseled out of the kind of stone they use for the most expensive kitchen counters, he began shaking hands with young assistants and producers. Some of them were women, and as I watched him make his way down the line, I noticed something odd in my coworkers' faces: a wince. Peterson had to notice, too, but he didn't let up. In fact, he seemed to be deriving some form of perverse pleasure from their pain. It's difficult, maybe even impossible, for me to describe the amount of force he used in these handshakes. The best I can do is to say it would shatter a wineglass but probably fall just short of turning wood into sawdust. As the scene played out, and the joy he gained showed no signs of abating, the sick feeling in the pit of my stomach got worse and worse. It was beyond uneasy.

All of us working on the show had a similar reaction. There were nervous grimaces from a few and odd glances from others as we attempted to assess the moment. We came to an unspoken agreement: this guy is wired differently, so let's make this quick.

One year later, Peterson's life started to unravel. Gruesome and frightening stories revealed that Peterson had aggressively whipped his four-year-old son. The details were hard to fathom: he used a stick that left bloody welts, even on his private parts, and jammed leaves down his son's throat as a means of punishment. It wasn't an isolated incident, either; more than one of Peterson's children, from several women, noted being frightened of their biological father.

Consider for a moment the nature of a four-year-old boy. He matures more slowly than girls and is generally more restless and distracted. He goes through odd but age-appropriate stages: biting, pushing, generally struggling to express himself. He's harder to potty train and more difficult to control as he grows slowly into his body. He's going through what experts call "an intuitive phase" where he is still learning about himself. During this phase, and up till eight years old, his little brain is struggling to understand the concept of consequences. He's probably way into bathroom humor, another sign that patience is not only necessary but crucial.

The details are disturbing, but they bear repeating: Peterson answered these challenges with beatings, with a switch, sometimes to the testicles, as a four-year-old boy screamed in terror. He suffocated and choked him briefly with dry leaves to muffle his pleas. It takes a certain kind of *sick* to dish out that level of punishment to a four-year-old child.

Let's be clear: this wasn't a slap on the behind of an eight-year-old who had petulantly pushed his sister off her bike. It was violence—violence coupled with anger and a weapon from perhaps the pound-for-pound strongest player in the league. It was administered to a terrified little boy who, at this point in his life, was probably just learning to form sentences.

You can only imagine what those sentences were in those dark moments. They were the words that struggled to get free in the pauses between screams.

PEOPLE SAY THEY WANT TO BE A MILLIONAIRE. IS WHAT THEY MEAN, "I WANT TO SPEND A MILLION DOLLARS"? BECAUSE THAT'S THE EXACT OPPOSITE OF BEING A MILLIONAIRE.

# A GOOD BET IS A TERRIBLE THING TO WASTE

**S**PORTS GAMBLING OCCUPIES an odd place in American society. The government actually has fewer restrictions on a guy who wants to peddle pornography on the Internet than it does on some poor sap in Iowa who wants to go online and bet an NFL teaser. The Bangbros porn site? Fine and dandy. Laying down a future bet on the Kansas City Royals? Whoa, just hold on there one minute, say the august members of the United States Senate, because that there bettin' business is making us awfully uncomfortable.

This fine country of ours will send an eighteen-year-old kid to the Middle East to fight a battle he never started or wanted and might not survive, but somehow taking NC State minus 6 against Boston College on a fall Saturday is an act that rises to the level of high crime.

I have a different perspective on this issue. I lived in Las Vegas for seven years and regularly discussed handicapping with the men who create the lines. It became clear they were no different from Wall Street analysts; instead of stocks or bonds or oil futures, their forte just happened to be games. They didn't offer opinions unless they were backed by provable, measurable data. If you think that decision makers like Oakland A's general manager–part owner Billy Beane and Houston Rockets GM Daryl Morey are trailblazers in the area of advanced metrics, you've never spent time with oddsmakers. They relied on trends and probabilities, a far cry from the paper-thin cotton-candy lead-with-your-heart analysis you hear on sports radio or television.

Look, I know there are bottom-feeders out there, skeevy dudes touting their "inside knowledge" and "Locks of the Week" on hyperventilating local radio commercials. They're so sure of themselves they'll give you one game free; just call the number now because it won't last long. They're a good match for the Twitter wiseguy wannabes who claim unblemished records through eleven weeks of an NFL season. You can spot the creeps and charlatans a mile away. They have nicknames like "the St. Louis Godfather" and claim locker room access to everything from hidden injuries to Andy Reid's latest game plan. Their job is to make you think every game is fixed, and they—and only they—are in on it.

But you have to understand something: these guys might have the biggest mouths and the most recognizable faces in the business, but they aren't the same guys who set the lines, and they're not the ones who build a durable reputation in the gaming world. Those guys, the pros, are the ones who establish themselves through hard work and dedication and research.

You know, sort of like every other business ever created.

The NFL has no need to publicly support sports gaming because the league already benefits greatly from it while remaining on the moral (read: silent) high ground. Clearly, though, if you look at the ratings for *Thursday Night Football* and *Monday Night Football*, even blowouts somehow manage to retain a large portion of their audience deep into the game. No other sport can make that boast. Why? Simple: people who bet over-under totals and play fantasy football keep their fingers off the remote to see if they will win cash before they crash. By the way, don't get me started on fantasy football. Don't think that's gambling? Then you'd better wake up. A company called FanDuel runs advertisements with fans claiming to win $450,000 in a single week. Tell me, please, how does one manage to win nearly a half million bucks in one week on football statistics *without* gambling?

There's a paradox at work. Legalizing sports gambling will create more regulation and therefore reduce corruption. And make no mistake: corruption and the threat of corruption definitely exist. Soccer and tennis matches held abroad have already been targets, to name two examples.

But I keep coming back to one fact: there has never been a Bernie Madoff or Michael Milken in sports gaming; no AIG or

WorldCom scam, either. Excess and outright thievery in the stock market are deemed *capitalism*—after all, the risk is just the system at work. That adorable feel-good movie *The Wolf of Wall Street* was nothing more than a little binge fun; the way things work if everything lines up for you in Manhattan. But across the Hudson, in Hoboken, New Jersey, be very scared of the nickel-and-dime bookie. He wins and loses money for those who have the discretionary cash to play, and winning or losing is determined by reasoned, fair analysis that results in competitive lines.

Most states have a lottery, where your odds are determined by pure, blind chance. When the jackpot rises to insane levels, how many people take big chunks of their money—money they can't afford to spend, in a lot of cases—and buy ticket after ticket based on multimillion-to-one odds? But that, somehow, is deemed to be perfectly okay—even harmless—by our government.

But sports gambling? Totally different story. It's seen as uncontrollable and invasive, a heroin-level addiction that will embed itself in our culture and transform every mailman and pharmacist into Fat Tony, pushing picks on unsuspecting civilians whose lack of self-control will inevitably lead to a quivering dependence on New York Rangers over-unders.

But what do I know? Maybe the government is right. Maybe sports gambling is the empire-crushing epidemic that the conspiracy theorists have been predicting. And our government did invent GPS, so there are times when it's a step or two—or even a quick right-hand turn—ahead of the game.

So let's strip it down to the studs and see how gaming works in this country:

There's this one city in the desert, uninhabitable before air-conditioning and riddled with a history of mob violence, where virtually any and every bet is fair game. There's a similar city in the East, one with all the charm of an all-night arm-wrestling tournament, that allows everything *but* sports gambling. The problem with Atlantic City, though, is that it can't seem to attract enough bettors to keep its casinos open. After that, we have national lotteries (Powerball), state lotteries, and scratch-off games (too many iterations to count), Indian casinos, riverboat gaming, horse tracks (where races are televised and celebrated nationally), and dog tracks (hey, sometimes people get bored and desperate). Some of these actually fund public schools.

And yet, despite this mishmash of rules and half-rules and government-sanctioned looks the other way, log on to www .placeabetonanactualgame.com and prepare to be handcuffed.

Here's a question: If the lines created by Vegas oddsmakers are so dubious, crafted by such obviously unscrupulous characters, then why are they used as *the expert opinion* by every major network and metropolitan newspaper? One percent of the gaming handle worldwide is derived from Las Vegas, but its "experts" are often used for information and advice during corruption cases. Federal authorities prosecuting both the 1994 Arizona State University and the 2009–2010 University of San Diego basketball point-shaving scandals sought expert (there's that word again) witnesses from Sin City's gaming industry.

This push-pull is nothing new. The people of the United States have always wrestled with the federal government when it comes to vices. Alcohol, marijuana, sex, and gambling are legislated with utmost rigidity until rules change because of public pressure or common sense, or—most pragmatically—politicians realize the potential to pry more tax revenue out of another industry. Of course, it is that last reason that serves as the impetus for a movement aimed at legitimizing sports gambling.

Well, sort of, anyway.

New Jersey governor Chris Christie is in favor of loosening the rules in his state, but it won't come without a fight—even though ESPN itself offers the occasional lines on college football games on the scroll at the bottom of the screen.

Oh, but what about all the people who will be preyed upon if sports gambling is legalized? The truth: sports gaming has better odds and a much smaller fee. Take our favorite comparison—lotteries—where the payout can be life-changingly enormous for that single winner among millions and millions, but the lottery "hold" is still 50 percent. That means the lottery keeps half your winnings, a fee that is ten times higher than anything that applies to any single NFL bet. Admittedly, you will never win $462 million on a single football bet, but your odds of at least doubling your money are incalculably greater.

I was vacationing in Vegas about five years ago, when I went to dinner with oddsmaker Brian Blessing. He was a regular listener to my show, and he contacted my producer to see if he could spend some time with me to pick my brain about the media. It worked for me, because I wanted to pick *his* brain on how lines are created and altered. Brian and I spent a dry, antiseptic ninety minutes discussing the minutiae of the oddsmaking business. We might as well have been discussing life insurance, providing that annuities wore helmets.

Before we even entered the restaurant, Brian pulled several sheets of paper out of his briefcase. They were filled with tiny lettering, the size normally found in the smallest print of a prescription bottle. Line after line was devoted to players and positions and statistics. Perhaps sensing my astonishment, Brian said, "Every player on every team in pro and college football has a point value. This is how I spend my summers."

I looked at him, my jaw slack.

"Fun, huh?" he asked.

This was his life: numbers, data, analyzing trends. He was not rich, but deep down inside, he knew there was one surefire way he could parlay his deep intellectual curiosity into something far more lucrative.

If only Bangbros was hiring.

# CONSTRUCTION CRITICISM

**M**Y FIRST THOUGHT was to blame the Ovaltine-and-peanut-butter smoothie my eight-year-old son drank before he got into the car. After all, it had to be *something* that got his mind racing like a Formula One engine, so why not a great night's sleep followed by an extra bolt of protein? Regardless of what caused it, we were barely buckled into the car when the questions started ricocheting off the back of my head:

"What makes a fire alarm sound like that?"

"How do they ship giraffes to a zoo?"

"Couldn't the president have handled ISIS better?"

At about that moment, I realized my answers couldn't be unthinking words that filled the space before our arrival at soccer practice. He was seeking serious and practical answers that could shape his ideas on issues he genuinely cared about. I had to put aside my usual role as Make Him Laugh Dad. I needed to quickly and permanently transform myself into Informed and Decisive Father.

Well, Make Him Laugh Dad was fun while it lasted.

Something else happened that day in the SUV: I started to wonder how to locate the line separating parental guidance from manipulation.

He once asked me about playing football, right about the time the NFL concussion topic was front and center. "I can't think of anyone who *died* playing it," I said. "But chronic pain will haunt you for the rest of your life if you play." He decided eventually on soccer.

Guidance? Or manipulation?

One steamy summer day, while I was driving to the mall with my daughter, we stopped at a light and saw a group of construction workers off to the right. Shirts off, working their asses off, getting roasted on a hot roof. You could see the sunburns forming in the time it took the light to go from red to green.

With precisely zero data to back my comments, and without any relationship with any of those men to assess their health or happiness, I said, "Have a plan in life, honey, or that could be you out there in that ninety-degree heat."

"What do you mean?" she asked.

"No little boy grows up wanting to bake on a roof. They want to be shortstops or firemen or inventors. You become in life what you plan for. So have a plan."

Guidance? Or manipulation?

Maybe I was just being the world's most judgmental prick. Or maybe, like my dad thirty-five years earlier, I was addressing a serious topic that could force my daughter to think about what her actions would mean years later.

The moment with my dad happened when I was thirteen or fourteen, shooting hoops by myself in the driveway. He came out to grab some firewood just as I launched a twenty-five-foot hook shot that bounced crazily off the rim.

He stood there, a couple of logs in his hand and a disgusted look on his face.

"Why would you *ever* take a shot like that? You wouldn't take that in a game, would you?"

As he headed back toward the house, I could see the grimace forming on his face. He looked over his shoulder and delivered his parting shot:

"Practice how you want to play."

That line landed squarely on the softest and most delicate part of my teenage psyche. As he walked slowly back into the house, I thought my dad saw me as a screw-off, nothing more. *Is that why he rarely comes to my games? Am I a disappointment to him?* It was painful, and years later, it remained potent.

How do we motivate without manipulating? How do we inspire kids without condemning others? How do we teach without injecting our personal biases?

Easy: you can't. Bias is everywhere. Opinion seeps into practically every sentence. You have to trust that your kids, like you, will gravitate toward the messages that inspire them.

My dad was never glib and rarely talkative. But his words—maybe because of their infrequency—carried uncommon power. With any luck, some of mine will, too. Unless, of course, my daughter always secretly dreamed of a long, hot career in construction.

# NASCAR NEEDS CRASHES OR FIGHTS TO BE INTERESTING. IT'S PRO WRESTLING WITH A WINDSHIELD.

# EYES WIDE SHUT

**S**LEEK BUT STURDY, cool without having to announce it, hip without trying too hard, the Peninsula is my favorite high-end hotel chain in this country. I was closing out a night with a friend at the rooftop bar at the Peninsula New York one perfect summer evening, when we struck up a conversation with a beautiful blonde. She was a stunning Polish beauty, and her English was good—or, I should say, good enough.

Several gin and tonics into our conversation, she opened up like a mob rat desperate to stay out of the joint. She told us she was a kept girl, as were many of her friends. They had places in the city provided by married Wall Street financiers and were routinely escorted to and from their homes in the Hamptons.

The names and firms were too precise to be contrived. Our skepticism dissolved amid her detailed descriptions. At one point, she challenged us to Google a vacation address she claimed was her destination the next morning. I did, and her recall was unimpeachable. She said her boyfriend's wife was traveling with friends in Europe for the week, so the place would be hers.

Listening to her, and double-checking her story, made me realize her words rose far above the level of cheap gossip. They were vivid and important, suggesting that some of the people in charge of the world's finances are greasier than aprons in a fast-food restaurant. This stuff felt like it mattered, and I was on a legitimate mission to excavate a small artifact of historical truth. Her leopard-print miniskirt didn't hurt the cause, either.

If you looked at her and heard her tell her story, you probably wouldn't have any reason to relate it back to sports. However, relating things back to sports is a feat of imagination I can always manage to accomplish, and in this case, her story empowered my belief that baseball's top beat writers were absolutely complicit in the sport's steroid scandal.

How's that for a connection? Hear me out.

The beat writer omertà was broken on June 3, 2002, by *Sports Illustrated* baseball writer Tom Verducci, who was the first to willingly pursue the story. Verducci's story, "Totally Juiced: Confessions of a Former MVP," didn't scorch the earth, but it opened up the conversation and brought the issue out of the darkest shadows. Verducci later admitted he knew, even before the season started, that steroid use would be the one story to dominate the sport in 2002. What Verducci did was not revolutionary: he listened to, and wrote about, players who were more than willing to talk. Shockingly, they were accommodating—if you only had the nerve to ask.

How many other baseball scribes could have reported and written similar stories? They heard the rumors and saw the evidence, right? Was Verducci the only observant writer covering the sport?

I contend the industry-wide silence is attributable to something far below the surface: the writers were covering an increasingly irrelevant sport (baseball) for an increasingly irrelevant industry (newspapers).

Two strikes, right? Criticism of baseball could be construed as being bad for two businesses. Don't look a gift horse and all that, right?

When in doubt, take the Roger Goodell route and claim plausible deniability.

On the drive back to Connecticut the morning after our encounter with the professional Polish mistress, I wondered how it was possible that a random visit to a New York bar could unearth names and firms and affairs from an industry to which I have little or no connection. And yet baseball writers, who travel with teams and often stay in the same hotels and spend hours and hours with ballplayers over the course of eight months every year, could not hear or validate one steroid story from the entire 1990s, a decade we now know was rife with PED use.

Seriously, not one?

Baseball's exhausting schedule demands a lot from writers.

They fill more space than their colleagues in other sports do: endless notes columns, daily game stories, Sunday specials. They are forced to update their blogs incessantly and tweet out everything from that day's lineup, to injury updates, to attendance figures. The job demands an acute level of attention to detail, as well as a thirst for anecdotes and interesting fillers. Information is currency.

Baseball, more than any other sport, lends itself to storytelling. Many of the top writers are considered the sharpest and most gifted in the sportswriting business. But on the steroids issue—perhaps the most important issue facing the sport in the past half century—all of these smart and observant and dedicated reporters suddenly had the investigative skills of Inspector Clouseau.

Just add up the numbers: ten years, 162 games per year, countless road trips, gallons and gallons of beer in hotel bars, thousands of discussions around the batting cage with players, coaches, scouts, and other writers. And through it all, amazingly enough, not one good tip on the surging power numbers and increasing size of the players.

It should be noted that Ken Caminiti, the source and subject of Verducci's story, had spoken openly and with ease on the topic of steroids. And Caminiti was not just another guy; he told Verducci he used steroids during his MVP season of 1996, when he hit .326 with forty homers and one hundred and thirty RBIs. In the previous nine seasons, Caminiti had hit more than twenty homers just once, making the 1996 season an outlier, a homing beacon for anyone steering their ship in the right direction. Verducci, who spoke with Caminiti for hours, later said that the former ballplayer was "completely unflinching and at ease, without hesitation." Any writer willing to dig just a bit had a willing informant, one willing to estimate that roughly half of all big-league players were using steroids.

Where were all those writers hanging out during the decade that steroids overtook their sport? I don't know—maybe the Hamptons, being pampered by their sugar daddies.

After Verducci's story was published, I did some exhaustive investigative research of my own: I made exactly one call to one big-league clubhouse manager I had known for a decade. With no hesitation, he confirmed a suspicion I had about Los Angeles Dodgers relief pitcher Eric Gagne's thirst for steroids (later confirmed through failed drug testing and MLB's official *Mitchell Report*) during a career that included a three-year stretch (2002–04) in which he averaged fifty saves a season. Nonchalantly but in significant detail, the clubbie told me it was common knowledge to anyone who bothered to pay attention. Among those who didn't: the eight Dodgers beat writers.

Could baseball writers argue that the historic nature and quirkiness of the sport create a romantic and protective reporting model? Could they argue that stimulants are a vital and accepted part of an outdoor summer sport—there is, after all, a rich and storied history—and they just thought some new-and-improved "greenies" (amphetamines, or pep pills) had made their way into the clubhouse?

Even if we accept both of those arguments—and it takes some mental gymnastics to do so—it still leaves a gigantic hole in the decade-long steroid cover-up. Baseball lives and dies by its obsessive reliance on numbers, and 'roids were skewing the numbers something fierce. And not just secondary numbers, but the types of numbers that define the very sport those writers love and strive to protect. Any suspicion—any suspicion at all—would have almost certainly led to some reporting. You know, for the good of the game and all.

I don't have recordings or DNA to prove that the Polish beauty actually had the affairs she claimed. Nor do I have recordings from baseball scribes to prove they heard stories about players being on the juice and ultimately refused to print them. What I do know is this: it widens the gap of trust between the public and the media when there is a sense that the country's most powerful pens swoop in to cover only the crises or scandals they're comfortable reporting.

If nothing else, those years of obliviousness proved what kind of game the writers would have had if *they'd* actually played the sport they covered. I'm picturing Dave Kingman or Rob Deer. You know, the guys best known for the big whiff. Only in this case, they never took the bat off their shoulder.

# TRADIN' PAINT AND WASTIN' TIME

**T**HE WAY MY SISTER, Marlene, and I remember it, our late father owned only three cars in his entire adult life. There was the International Harvester Jeep, in which he took us for long Sunday drives on the beach when we were kids. There was the Buick Riviera, which arrived at roughly the same time as his mid-life crisis. And finally there was the brown GMC truck, which may have set some kind of domestic record for being driven the most consecutive miles without being cleaned.

My dad never spent a single solitary moment in a garage fixing any one of his three cars, and so I—as his son—never developed anything resembling a fascination with automobiles. They're the same as an oven or a refrigerator: a part of my life strictly for their utility. They're transportation, nothing more. The whole romantic idea of hitting the open road never blossomed inside my young soul, probably because it was stifled by the smell inside the pickup. My idea of romance when it comes to cars is rooted in practicality: the longer you drive one without a payment, the more you beat the system.

This probably makes it easy to understand why, after twenty-five years covering sports, NASCAR is the only popular one I can't begin to comprehend. I'm not trying to deny its popularity; it was on network television for years, and *Sports Illustrated* once predicted that its popularity would soar to NFL levels. Advertisers seem engaged and willing to spend. The grandstands at the tracks are often full.

And yet in my entire adult life, I have known one person who likes NASCAR. Well, sort of likes it, anyway. I'll call him Chris, mostly because that's his name, and this needs to be authentic. He tried to explain the sport once, so I do have a handle on some of the basics.

Before I go any further, though, I need to clarify a few things. There are many things I do not like and yet understand why they are popular despite my indifference. To name a few: watches, cowboy boots, science-fiction movies, pet birds, ski trips, the Pro Bowl, loud engines, and other human beings. I understand those things. I get why they're popular. I've even questioned why I don't like them.

But NASCAR? Man, that's a head-scratcher.

Millions of Americans, traditionally on oppressively hot days, jam into grandstands, plop themselves onto hard bench seats, and cheer wildly—hour after excruciating hour—for cars that are often so far away they exist only in the imagination. These fast cars jostle for position endlessly, the difference between them reduced to an almost imperceptible level by increased regulations. The cars sometimes stop briefly—no longer than a minute—to get more fuel and fresh tires. These fans, enraptured by what amounts to a glorified trip to Jiffy Lube, cheer that, too.

Fans have favorite drivers inside those cars, but you can't see much of them during a race. I discovered, with Chris's help, that fans are also intensely loyal to the car itself. Ford, Chevy, and Dodge are the big three NASCAR automakers, and each has its own cheering section on race day. That's fascinating, and a little troubling, when you say it out loud: fans standing and cheering for Big Detroit and internal combustion.

They don't even do that at the factories.

These races last hours. Most of the stands are uncovered, which means the fans sit in direct sunlight the entire time. And it's loud—oh, Lord, is it ever loud. Sometimes there are crashes, which seems like it would make it more interesting. At least break up the left-turn/tire-change monotony. Mostly, though, there are not crashes. It's just driving and more driving, most of it taking place off in the distance, which you have to admit lacks a certain energy. James Spader once starred in a movie about rooting for car crashes. He called it *Crash*. I know: it bored *me*, too.

I've attended two Daytona 500s, and somewhere between the unrelenting noise and the noxious smell of gasoline, I might have passed out. Or maybe I didn't—I can't remember—but I do know I have no idea which driver or which make of car won either race. It seems like his name was Denny. Yeah, Denny sounds right. His fans were almost all badly sunburned, which—come to think of it—could have been avoided. I distinctly recall sun being in the forecast.

NASCAR isn't as popular as it was ten years ago, according to statistics compiled by ESPN research. Geez, that would be a painstaking job, wouldn't it? Researching NASCAR's popularity? I think I might prefer to count nails all day. Seriously, how long could a person stay in that job?

There's no reason to root for NASCAR's demise. That's not my goal here. Frankly, I probably wouldn't know if it vanished, anyway. There's a race somewhere today or tomorrow. To each his own. Fans will pour into the track and cheer.

And they'll cheer for a guy they can't see and an automaker they don't work for and a car that's miles away. I don't know how to explain any of it. Gasoline fumes? That's my best guess. I don't think my dad would have understood any of it.

# THE CUSTOMER
## ISN'T ALWAYS RIGHT—
# SOMETIMES
## THE CUSTOMER IS A JERK!

# LOUD, PROUD, AND DEAD WRONG

**C**ONSIDER FOR A MOMENT a most common occurrence: men arguing. Note the body language and the size of the men and the way the volume fluctuates as the argument wears on. You will see a certain dynamic play out with alarming frequency. The men who are physically imposing almost always get louder and more threatening. Their argument doesn't become any more convincing—in other words, they don't get any smarter—but they use their size to fill the leadership void.

This is precisely what happened with the Miami Dolphins during the 2013 season. They provided the perfect conditions for a field experiment to determine whether an NFL locker room, like nature itself, abhors a vacuum.

All of the variables were in place. The Dolphins lacked a noteworthy, domineering head coach. They were playing with a rookie quarterback. They had no perennial All-Pro alpha-male personality who could command respect and set the direction for the entire team. As has been the case for some time, they appeared to be a rudderless ship.

From a purely sociological standpoint, what took place shouldn't have been so surprising. Offensive tackle Jonathan Martin quit the team midseason, a decision that turned out to be connected to vile, racists texts he'd been receiving from teammate Richie Incognito. A longtime creep, someone who had been kicked out of two colleges for antisocial behavior, a fixture atop the election results for NFL's dirtiest player, Incognito possessed all the charm of an arms dealer.

And yet, in this locker room, amid this wobbly franchise, the veteran Incognito was allowed to take command. He became the leading voice, the void filler, the domineering personality who dictated the team's path.

This seems like a football thing—right?—or at least a sports thing. Workplaces that rely on machismo and ego are fertile soil for the loud-mouthed, follow-me-or-fight-me mentality espoused by Incognito.

Surely this dynamic couldn't exist in the more civilized parts of the world, could it?

As it turns out, the Republican Party is conducting its own experiment. The GOP is being run—or at least mobilized—by a steady chorus of Sir Scream-a-Lots, with an assist from fearmongers selling worst-case scenarios like street-corner drug dealers. The volume level, roughly equivalent to the inside of a jet engine, has drowned out the centrists and those with reasonable right-leaning views.

According to the Pew Research Center, 71 percent of Americans support raising the minimum wage to more than $10 an hour. Universal background checks on all gun purchases? That's supported by 81 percent. Research from ABC News and the *Washington Post* indicates that 58 percent of Americans—and growing—support gay marriage. Climate change is acknowledged by 73 percent. Those overwhelming numbers indicate that many conservatives hold those very same beliefs, but you'd never know it from listening to them. The far right, with its Incognito-level bullying and volume, has silenced the more moderate faction of the GOP.

Again, remember what these numbers prove: many registered Republicans are voting for these "left-leaning" ideas. Why? Well, that goes directly to my main point: these are *not* left-leaning ideas. They are commonsense conclusions reached by a vast majority of Americans. The vocal minority has managed to cast these views as extreme. In the process, it has hijacked reason.

As a result, if you so much as acknowledge the existence of climate change, if you accept the empirical evidence of rising sea levels and the increase in historically devastating storms, you are labeled a radical and a socialist by the loudest voices of the GOP. It makes no difference that roughly 97 percent of board-certified climatologists and internationally acclaimed scientists agree. The leadership void exists, and volume wins.

This is the end result of having the wrong people controlling the microphone. When the agenda is driven by the loudest and most threatening, intellect and reason get lost amid the noise and the bluster. The power of the schoolyard-bully dynamic, capable of upsetting an NFL franchise and disrupting an entire political party, is undeniable and more than a little frightening.

Keep one rule in mind when you find yourself dealing with *loud*: it's never right. You get the same result from the loudest guy at the bar, the biggest screamer on television, and the band that leaves you partially deaf for days on end. The louder it gets, the less it delivers.

# FOOD AND WHINE

**T**HE LOUD PROCLAMATIONS coming from the table behind me got my immediate attention.

The lady doing the proclaiming was probably well intentioned. She was definitely proud of herself. She regaled her tablemates—and most of the restaurant—with tales of the many and fulfilling ways her recent divorce had catapulted her into a new, more spiritual life.

She had apparently reached a new level of consciousness. Material items no longer have any meaning, she said. As I sat with my back to her, I learned that her wondrous transformation was so complete it now included a totally organic diet.

The irony of this Zen-like epiphany hit hard when she and her first-ballot Hall of Fame boob job—creating a Rio Grande Valley of cleavage—walked past me as she left the restaurant.

Yeah, she was *way* into that whole natural thing, except for the six pounds of silicone implanted in her chest. And trust me when I tell you she walked in a manner that indicated serious pride. She advertised herself; that was obvious to anyone without cataracts.

By all means, inflate away. I'm all for physical and financial endowments of almost any kind, but her performance in the minutes leading up to my introduction to her surgical sisters leads me to a larger point.

Can the leaders and proponents of the current organic lifestyle movement scale back the rhetoric? Can we stop pretending that an affinity for brussels sprouts and green tea is some sort of revolution? Can we go back to the days when enjoying a kale salad wasn't an endorsement of an eco-friendly political platform?

I liked the "revolution" better when it was called "eating a little healthier."

Gone are the halcyon days of personal experimentation, when humans tested out a new diet or cause in the privacy of their own homes and kept their damned mouths shut about it. Those days, sadly, are history. The way it works now, a full commitment is required, involving marches, weekend rallies, a wardrobe makeover, and an almost religious disdain for anyone who resides outside your camp. Maybe it started with the "Free Love" movement, or perhaps "Save the Whales," but now "Go Green" currently shares the hippest cubicle with the organic-or-die crowd. Shopping for basil and sweet potatoes is now a lifestyle.

First off, if you believe the studies, nobody is really sure that eating an organic diet even has a nutritional advantage over a more conventional diet. Yes, grass-fed beef is better for you, but the sugar in the Whole Foods sugar cookie is the harmful ingredient, not the preservatives the manufacturer has helpfully kept out of the process. There's also a rarely discussed downside of a potential dreamworld where everybody consumes only organic food: we'd have to cut down more than ten million more square miles of forest to accomplish that mythical agricultural nirvana. Golf courses might be more efficient uses of land.

Listen, there's a more cynical side of this issue, one that goes beyond clean living and good health. Like any well-intentioned idea, if it's profitable, corporations will seize the opportunity to grab a piece of the market share. The most important and lasting consequence of the organic food boom is that major grocery store chains will lose customers if they don't offer supposedly healthier choices. Despite that, the organic food movement now sounds like one giant feel-good sales pitch rather than anything based on science or reality.

How am I not supporting a local farmer *somewhere* if I eat two bananas that I bought at Walmart? How does more expensive organic food help people, especially kids, who can't afford conventional food right now? And have you ever tried to drink organic cranberry juice or use hemp toilet paper?

I'm not coming down on every Saturday farmer's market. It's not an indictment of a cleaner diet or greater environmental awareness. Nobody on earth enjoys a good bowel cleansing more than my family, but amid the endless pursuit of an elevated eating experience, I feel compelled to stand up and show my proud support for the act of eating so much sausage lasagna that it forces me to unbutton my jeans. Would I offend the almond butter zealots if I strongly recommend a dozen hot wings? Have you ever known anyone who becomes sadder after devouring a plate of chicken nachos? Are you aware that eating too many carrots—organic or otherwise—can cause your skin to turn orange? You don't hear that shit about Cracker Jack, do you?

Okay, I'll admit it: I just included that last one to piss off a few vegans.

By all means, pound that mango smoothie. Knock down several helpings of butternut squash tonight, and I will gladly join you for a helping of antioxidants afterward. I won't feel more spiritual or more in tune with the environment, but there's a good chance I might feel the urge to consume a big bowl of factory-created chips and salsa to fill my stomach.

It'll probably happen about an hour later, and I'll eat those free of guilt and unattached to a higher cause. And I promise I won't feel the need to tell the world around me that it carries any greater meaning.

# I DON'T WANT TO LIVE IN A CITY WHERE AN ATHLETE MAKES IT BETTER. I WANT THE SCHOOLS TO MAKE IT BETTER.

# THE POLITICS OF EVERYTHING, THE EVERYTHING OF POLITICS

**I** **HAD NO INTEREST IN POLITICS** as a teenager. I can say with near certainty that I was probably either bouncing a ball or throwing one while a lot of important worldly events took place without me. Maybe if I had paid closer attention, I could have pinpointed the exact moment when every personal decision, from paper-or-plastic to Swiss-or-cheddar, indicated where someone's belief system lands on the political spectrum.

What you think is appropriate food for school lunches is a political issue. Come down against potato chips, and, well, good luck defending yourself against charges that you think Michelle Obama should run the world. The kind of car you drive is a political issue—of course it is, because everyone knows the SUV in your driveway is a sign that you have no concern whatsoever for trees, birds, fish, ocean levels, or your fellow human beings.

Even your take on whether the government should allocate funds to stop ebola—ebola, for shit's sake!—is a partisan issue.

Any opinion you have on the weather—*on the freakin' weather*—is a referendum on your politics. Thirty years ago, your mother could say, "It's a little unseasonably warm for April, isn't it?" and nobody would bat an eye. Now, though, there's no such thing as an innocuous comment. Nothing is off-limits. An offhand remark about the weather could trigger verbal fireworks.

"Oh, you think it's warm for April, do you? What are you really trying to say? I bet you voted for Obama, too. You know he's ruined this country, don't you? Let me tell you about my friend: he lost his job. It doesn't matter that he stopped going to work and could be a tad intolerant racially—seriously, who isn't when you get right down to it? It's irrelevant that he admitted to referring to certain female coworkers as 'Sweet Yummy Desserts' in the elevator—he admitted that was poor judgment. Wait, where was I? Oh, yeah: Obama has ruined this great land, stomped all over the Constitution, and wants to institute Sharia law. You know he's from Kenya, don't you?"

This is our world, folks. Everything is political. And—unlike the climate—it's not changing anytime soon.

How in the hell did we get here? How did your views on evolution become linked to your opinion on fracking? How did your thoughts on American military intervention in unstable Middle Eastern countries come to indicate whether you're more or less likely to prefer organic free-range chicken?

I'm not completely sure, but I do know the true beauty of this mess: you can blame either side and be equally right and equally wrong. Flip a coin and shake your head at the mess we've created.

And I also know this: the whole operation has been created, escalated, and propagated by good old-fashioned American capitalism. Taking a side and driving it home, over and over, makes economic sense. Far left and far right have gained traction on television, despite statistical evidence that more than 60 percent of the electorate claims to hug the middle.

The media itself has become a political issue. Your viewing habits—the networks you watch and when you watch them—say something about your political bent. It's an emotional appeal; if the people who are calling the shots can make their agenda your agenda, they win.

Television is different—almost a separate entity from the rest of what we consider media. Let's break the media into four groups:

- Social media

- Written word (newspapers, magazines, books)

- Radio

- Television

Each medium relies on a key element to drive interest: traffic, or ratings. Cleverness, amid Twitter's space limitations, can draw a large audience. The value of the written word is driven by intelligence. The best radio performers capture attention through storytelling. And television? Well, TV is an entirely different animal.

Just be dynamic.

This isn't limited to the delivery of political views, or news with a political slant. Compile a list of the top dramas and sitcoms over the last fifty years, and you'll come to a clear understanding of what I mean. There's not one that didn't rely on a certain dynamism to make it work. There was the chemistry of *M*A*S*H* and *Seinfeld*, the writing of *Cheers* and *Mad Men*, the robust on-screen performances of *Breaking Bad* and *The Sopranos*. The best television jumps through the screen and grabs you. It's far more immediate and visceral.

You don't even have to like the characters; sometimes, in fact, it's better if you don't. You don't have to be able to relate to them or respect them. The only mortal sin: dullness. If the characters are perceived to be boring—or even thoughtful or reasonable—they disappear.

On television, whether it's politics or sports or even a food channel, it pays to explode. If you're odd or bizarre, all the better. Unpredictability sells. In a galaxy of five hundred channels, sexy trumps subtle. Production costs can be prohibitive, so it's more cost effective to stage a raging debate, preferably with wild accusations made in rising voices. If you're shrewd enough, or loud enough, you can distance yourself from the other striving cast members. All for the low monthly rate of two or three reasonably attractive fast talkers. Or chefs—take your pick.

Some see it as nothing less than the end of civilization, but is there a chance it could be healthy? I'm here to make the case that it is.

Best-selling author Walter Isaacson expressed a similarly counterintuitive opinion on the issue of privacy in his book *The Innovators: How a Group of Hackers, Geniuses, and Geeks Created the Digital Revolution*. In Isaacson's opinion, the explosion and advancement of technology have created a fear that we have lost all privacy and, along with it, our ability to escape not only the distractions of our smartphones and computers but also the prying eyes of constant surveillance. Increasingly, people have chosen to make their worlds public, sharing their vacation photos on Facebook and their opinions on Twitter. Isaacson looked at this growing phenomenon and came away with a less fearful take: With everyone's views and lives so public, it forces us to be more thoughtful and respectful. The penalty for violating those tenets—public scorn—is more serious than ever before.

Anonymous venom can be a powerful tool, but the second it becomes public, *you* become the tool. Isaacson noted that the *Huffington Post*'s decision to force its commenters to go public by using their Facebook identities caused a drastic cut in the number of incendiary comments. That should have surprised precisely nobody.

Television is personal because it comes directly into our homes, but how much influence does it really carry? When the worth of a belief system or a sporting event becomes intrinsically tied to its television ratings, are we overreacting to the medium's power and reach? On the flip side, are the loudest and most popular clown shows actually hurting the causes they promote?

Let me make this personal.

As Fox News and conservative radio have exploded in popularity, I have been a consumer of both. How is it, then, that I have simultaneously become *less* conservative in my voting patterns and everyday thought processes?

Is it possible that watching the often-lopsided commentary from the Red State Network has had the opposite of its intended effect? Could its occasional pandering to its older and fearful base have awakened me to the necessity for more nuanced coverage? Could Fox News be enlightening me rather than swaying me? Am I alone in this?

Has the occasional bombast really enriched the conservative movement? Couldn't I argue that it's now angrier and more splintered, with factions being created within factions?

Sports television has grown in a manner that parallels the growth of the politically motivated news networks. There are now more than thirty networks with around-the-clock programming, much of it featuring conflict-driven debate shows. And you know what's happening? Growth, steady and unending. All those bad things predicted by the hand-wringing critics just aren't happening. Media folks who never had wealth and attention now have both. And, more importantly, the increased visibility and popularity of sports programming has advanced a lot of traditionally underserved constituencies:

- In the past ten years, an increasing number of minority and female athletes have become more visible and empowered. They are now co-owners and key investors in pro franchises and sports apparel companies. They're no longer simply athletes or employees— they're bosses. Women's sports have undergone an exponential rise in popularity and exposure over this period.

- There is far more equality in coaching and management at both the collegiate and professional levels, and I would argue that this can be traced directly to the increase in diversity in the media.

- More of those talking heads shouting at one another are actually shouting about topics that nobody was addressing twenty years ago.

- The conversation regarding payment of college athletes, steered by legal and media questioning, has gained traction. In fact, it could finally result in the National Collegiate Athletic Association (NCAA) enacting rules to provide stipends.

- Rampant drug use has been uncovered in cycling and baseball, and the exposure has materially altered the rules. After decades of dangerous and unchecked cheating, both sports are cleaner than before.

- The NFL has been forced to acknowledge the dangers of concussions and will eventually distribute more than $1 billion to support former players who have been affected.

- Hazing has been not only reduced but also criminalized. Bullying by coaches, often brought to light through video footage, has undergone a massive shift in public opinion.

Look, there's no denying the existence of sports shows and narratives that make us cringe—the seemingly endless Tim Tebow national crisis is one—but it's unrealistic to expect nonstop, nirvana-level content in any industry.

Is every new technological application used solely for good? Of course not, but it has intensified competition and fostered innovation, which will eventually push the silly and harmful stuff to the margins. You know, just like in any industry.

On the topic of parenting, my wife often says, "Be a great example or, if nothing else, a horrible warning. Both can work." That's exactly what I see happening on my television. The yelling and the conflict might be a horrible warning, but it works by creating smarter and more enlightened debates. It must—if for no other reason than to quiet and disarm the screamers.

All growth, whether personal or professional, arises out of discomfort. Artists don't wake up in the morning to see the skies open and a divine hand guide them through a masterpiece in a matter of minutes. It's the pain that makes the painting.

And yes, television is sometimes just a shiny object that attracts those who seek primitive entertainment. It also partners on the virtual dance floor with a force that empowers individuals and causes that never knew they could have it.

The trick is knowing where to look. The remote gives power to people on both ends of it. Use yours to find the good.

# FEW COMPLAINTS

**O**N A COOL SATURDAY NIGHT in the northeastern corner of our most northwestern state, notoriously private Gonzaga University basketball coach Mark Few allowed me a brief glimpse into his personal Valhalla. As we sat on the deck of his stunning cliff-side home near Spokane, Washington, we shared beers, laughs, and the kind of inside information I can't repeat (but will use for years to come to provide context and buttress my arguments on college basketball).

For a hoops junkie, this was an all-time fix. There were miles of pine trees below us, and—when we weren't talking or laughing—a complete silence from a perch that felt like the top of the world. Every breath of crisp, clean air hammered home the same point: this felt like a magical basketball rejuvenation center.

I told Few, "I doubt Ben Howland ever had this view when

he coached at UCLA," and, after we had a good laugh, followed it by wondering out loud if Few had ever been tempted to make a run at a higher-profile job.

Few reacted like I had suggested something unnatural. "Why would I?" he asked me. "Instead of trying to win twenty-eight games a year like the rest of us, at those other places you deal with additional layers of needless stuff. You even have to answer questions if you don't land the four- and five-star recruits everybody's been reading about for three or four years. Here, we don't pay attention to that stuff. No, thanks."

When it comes to coaching jobs, perception rarely interferes with reality.

What is Few missing by staying in Spokane? It's hard to tell. He no longer has to fly commercial; a rotating set of private jets from boosters takes care of that. His drive to work is ten minutes in an area with no traffic jams or prying media. There are biking and jogging trails just outside his door—perfect for his lifestyle. His job produces less stress than the so-called "big-time" jobs; a weaker conference virtually guarantees not only a spot in March Madness but also a nice seed.

And, oh, by the way, Mark Few is in the midst of a ten-year contract.

Compare it to the marquee job in the most popular American sport: head coach in the NFL. On average, the NFL head coach makes only slightly more money than Few. He must coach in a larger city with more big-city issues and an aggressive, attacking media. He must coach in a league where every team is well funded, and no team—theoretically, at least—has a huge recruiting advantage.

In college, you're allowed to build a system that rewards you tomorrow with every win today. Top programs such as Gonzaga win so often and play on television so regularly that they begin to recruit themselves. There are no legislative or league-imposed limitations on how dominant you can become. The more you win, the more you're seen, and the easier the whole thing becomes.

There's work involved, sure, but it's kind of like the captain clicking on autopilot: you still have to pay attention, just not as intently.

In the NFL, the better your team plays, the lower your pick in the draft—pretty much the opposite of the college-hoop model. Playoff teams in the NFL have free-agent limitations, and salary caps force unpopular personnel decisions. The stated goal of the league—parity—sounds charming if you're in the commissioner's office, but it's not as appealing to the coach who just led his team to the Super Bowl and knows the league would prefer someone else to take his place the next year.

During our night on the porch, the wiry Few had just returned from up the road at beautiful Hayden Lake, Idaho, where he water-skied with his kids all afternoon. He was wearing a Maui visor and talking about how much he loves that lake before shifting excitedly to the topic of an incoming transfer from the University of Southern California. From where I sat, this coach was the poster boy for physical and mental health.

Contrast that with the overweight, sleep-deprived, chronically cranky NFL lifer storming hypertensively along a sideline near you. As of 2015, just nine of thirty-two head coaches have been with the same team for at least five years. Job security is so tenuous in the NFL that one coach, San Francisco's Jim Harbaugh, was nearly traded for a player after the 2013 season and was fired after a poor 2014 season despite leading his team to three straight NFC championship games and one Super Bowl in four seasons.

That's all true. Every word of it. Which makes you wonder if international drug running offers more job security.

Looking around at college coaches, one thing becomes abundantly clear: these are happier, healthier people than their professional counterparts. They have more job security, more wins, and more control over both their present and their future. Nick Saban, head coach at the University of Alabama, is sixty-four and looks ten years younger. Oklahoma's Bob Stoops, Georgia's Mark Richt, Washington's Chris Petersen, and Stanford's David Shaw are almost strangely youthful. Some NFL coaches, on the other hand, start to look like old driftwood around their midfifties.

During an appearance on my radio show, Duke University basketball coach Mike Krzyzewski—Coach K—offered up this nugget: "Every year on a college campus, there are new young people—and new ideas—arriving. It energizes you. You have to keep up with the new technology, and I think it keeps me younger."

As the sun set over a distant hill, Few's parents brought us a pan of freshly baked brownies. I glanced down at my phone to see a text from a friend. It was a link to a story about the coach of his favorite football team. The guy was on the hot seat, his job in jeopardy, the end undoubtedly near.

And the most amazing thing about it? Football season hadn't even started yet.

# THE QUIETER
# THE ROOM,
## THE DEEPER THE THOUGHTS.

# A GOOD FELLA IS
# HARD TO FIND

**T**HE FIRST TIME I saw Ray Liotta on-screen—I'm guessing it was in the 1986 film *Something Wild*—I immediately detected a presence that demanded my attention. Even among other gifted actors, he could own a scene without even talking. He was a force of nature when all he was doing was standing and staring.

Here was a fascinating paradox: the kind of guy whose personality seemed steady enough for you to introduce him to a friend, but whose internal wiring was strung so tightly you could see him strangling someone for being impolite. Even his laugh—a mirthless staccato—sounds like it emanates from a dark place; maybe a humorless childhood. Or maybe he's a good enough actor to create impressions that take my mind to gloomy places full of secrets and half-truths.

One day I was waiting to join a group for lunch at a bar in

Beverly Hills when Liotta approached me. Here came those same steely eyes and unforced intensity—it was more than a little disconcerting. He shook my hand and told me he enjoyed my work. He couldn't have been more complimentary, or intimidating. I didn't dare look away; I wanted to show respect, but more importantly, I was hoping not to piss him off. I'd seen all the movies; I could see my lifeless body being tossed dismissively into someone's carpeted trunk.

Liotta's physical presence—he's just six feet tall but somehow outsized—reminded me of the time I bumped into Hall of Fame quarterback Dan Marino at the London hotel on West Fifty-Seventh Street in New York City. The lobby was filled with well-dressed, handsome people, and within that group, Marino felt like the most important person in the room.

It's hard to define what I'm getting at here. It is not a single quality but a combination of qualities wrapped into one. It's *presence* and *poise* and *charisma*, but any one of those taken independently just doesn't do it justice.

ESPN commentator Trent Dilfer, a former NFL quarterback who now mentors some of the best young ones, calls these indefinables "Dude Qualities" and believes firmly that they're essential for dominance at the position. Maybe I should call mine "Liotta Principles," because Dilfer and I are speaking the same language with different reference points.

Employing a metric combining "Dude Qualities" with "Liotta Principles," I could have predicted the careers of Ben Roethlisberger and Alex Smith based on my encounters with them at a golf event more than a decade ago in Simi Valley, California. Smith was the number one pick in the 2007 draft, and yet he was so quiet he almost disappeared into the rack of golf shirts. He was modest and conscientious and all the things I hope my son will be at age twenty-one. Roethlisberger, in contrast, was not a man bothered by subtlety. He didn't shake my hand—he seized it. He was large and confident, immediately at ease with the celebrities around him. He was the least-known person in the room at that time, but it was clear he felt he belonged. He led his foursome—three older men and him—out of the pro shop like a commanding officer.

You could see that same confidence as he led his Pittsburgh Steelers teams to a pair of Super Bowls in 2008 and 2010. There's an obvious willingness to improvise in the biggest spots and take risks at precisely the times others would scale back. It's the same mentality that got him into trouble off the field—two sexual assault allegations, leading to a four-game suspension in 2010. It's the kind of trouble that has never found Alex Smith. Clearly, Ben's belief in Ben is unmistakable, even in the few minutes I spent with him. It was Liotta-esque.

You can get away with being less cocky than Roethlisberger if you play other positions in other sports. Liotta Lite can make it as a position player in baseball, where the action can be limited to four at-bats. Hockey stars are rarely on the ice for longer than the standard ninety-second interval, which limits their overall impact on a game. Even in basketball, execution and teamwork generally beat prolific individual scoring.

And then we get to football. Football is different because of one dominant position: quarterback. He touches the ball seventy-five times a game and controls tempo, egos, and play calls for more than three hours. The best ones elevate the play of every player in the huddle and even help the defense by keeping it off the field for long stretches.

A quarterback, to be truly successful, has to go Full Liotta.

At the end of the 2014 season, nine NFL coaches were fired. All nine of those teams lacked an experienced, elite quarterback. In college football, Mack Brown was run out of Texas and Will Muschamp was fired in Florida for many reasons that were excusable and one that wasn't: a series of misses at quarterback. It's the one spot on the field you can't afford to screw up.

How important, and rare, are great quarterbacks? Of the sixty-two drafted from 2010 through 2014, I contend that only one—Andrew Luck of the Indianapolis Colts—is a true franchise star. Only a handful of others, such as Detroit's Matthew Stafford from the '09 class, have shown signs of rising to that level before they dropped back into that vast middle ground between solid and good enough to get you into the playoffs most years.

To be more blunt, it looks like this: the best and most experienced football executives in the country, fully understanding the importance of a great QB for their team's success and their own employment, have about the same success rate as a blindfolded golfer.

A quick look at the job requirements shows that it's harder to be one than to find one.

Wanted: elite NFL quarterback.

Necessary skills: a good amount of mobility, but not so much that it becomes your defining quality; intelligence, but not so much that you overthink; confidence, but not so much that it comes across as arrogance; the vague but know-it-when-you-see-it "It" factor, but not so much that it becomes an effort to make everyone aware of it.

In short, you need what Big Ben had that day I met him.

To take this a bit further, and to underscore just how damned hard it is to draft and develop a superstar at the position, I put the last sixty-two drafted quarterbacks, spanning the five-year period beginning in 2010, into four categories:

- **franchise (can carry a team to the Super Bowl)**—Andrew Luck;

- **faux franchise (can get to a Super Bowl, with lots of help)**—Russell Wilson, Matthew Stafford;

- **false franchise (capable of doing enough to fool fans about Super Bowl potential)**—Andy Dalton, Cam Newton, Ryan Tannehill; and

- **fo'get it**—the other fifty-six.

There is very little to suggest an end to this dreadful trend. Increasingly, the NFL is a pressurized environment with demanding owners leaning on impatient general managers who give coaches an ultimatum: play the fresh new star quarterback the fans want to see—or else.

Oh, and you'd better win while you're doing it.

All of a sudden, a three-year developmental process becomes a nine-week crash course. The process can devour even a top prospect with some of the essential job skills. Have you ever met a twenty-two-year-old capable of being the face of a billion-dollar franchise while learning the ropes of its most demanding position?

Roethlisberger didn't do it alone, either. His success can be attributed in great measure to the organization that drafted him. If he hadn't been brought along persistently and smartly by the respected Pittsburgh Steelers, he could have possessed all the necessary job requirements and *still* ended up as another failed footnote.

You know, sort of like what might have happened to Ray Liotta back in 1990 if he'd been cast in *Pretty Woman* instead of *Goodfellas*.

# LIFE CYCLE

**I**T'S **HARD TO THINK** of anyone who went from national icon to unconditional dirtbag more thoroughly than Lance Armstrong. It's an unexpected consequence of the speed of modern information: from cancer-survivor superhero to shady drug peddler in a matter of hours. That's the world we live in—fast to the top; even faster to the bottom—and while Lance is unique in his own way, he's not alone. NBC's Brian Williams can tell you how it's possible to go from respected newsman to bullshit artist over the course of one viral afternoon.

The truth is something we all profess to want, and both men avoided it whenever possible. The difference lies in their lines of work. Williams is a journalist and is paid to have integrity. Armstrong is an athlete—so, not so much.

Lance is a remarkable case study, because a funny thing happened to Sir Lies-a-Lot as soon as we all came to the foregone conclusion that he cheated his way to seven Tour de France titles from 1999 to 2005. The man started being really, painfully honest, and we decided we didn't like that, either.

In an interview a year after his public spanking, Armstrong was asked once again about his drug use. And he admitted, in typical Lance fashion, that if he could reverse time and go back to his glory days, he would do it all over again. With that steely, clear-eyed, I-dare-you-to-hate-me look, he said that the culture in cycling was so dirty—the steroids, the hanging IV bags of EPO, the whole traveling-pharmacy aspect of the Tour—that he didn't think he would change a thing.

Oh, and how media scolds responded. "He doesn't get it," they bleated in unison. "We're all being played for fools once again."

But maybe, just maybe, Lance really does get it.

I'm going to preface this by saying I'm not defending or excusing Armstrong. I'm not suggesting he's a victim of circumstances or a misunderstood genius. Instead, I'm going to attempt to place him within a context that might shed some light on decisions—especially socially unacceptable decisions—made by people who crave the spotlight.

Let's start by saying that every society has certain strengths, truths, and liabilities. In the United States, celebrity life emanates a power that can't be measured. It takes a regular life and turns it into an endless procession of valets, freebies, and perks. You get lifelong access to power and opportunity. Our system, more than probably any other country's, is built to allow the famous to enjoy the riches and luxuries of their position. Syria doesn't have anything close to Kanye West, and there are no Kardashians in Poland.

We also have short memories. We're so busy keeping up with the next scandal that we often forget about the last one. That gives the fallen star an opportunity for reinvention. Former criminals become TV hosts and expert analysts. Former reckless rock stars reform themselves into savvy business experts. Famously destructive drug users write best-selling children's books.

We buy just about every second act, but none of it happens unless you were once a star.

Armstrong now has two life experiences that no cyclist can ever match. He was once American royalty, flying on private jets and directing a team of people to attend to his every need while he soaked up the insatiable adulation of an adoring public. And he'll have that again, in time, once he reshapes his image.

He's still got it pretty good. He has his closest and most loyal friends, a girlfriend who probably reveres him, and a dog that still runs to the door. I'm guessing he sleeps eight hours a night and works a lot less than the rest of us and has more free time to enjoy life. He's not seven feet tall like an NBA player, so he can put on some glasses and a baseball cap and temporarily disappear into the fabric of society. He rides a bike in his spare time, and the media doesn't spend much time staking out single-track trails or the shoulders of mountain roads.

Again, I'm not defending his actions, but there's a vital truth about lying: we all do it, and pretty frequently. A study claims that 60 percent of us can't go ten minutes without telling some form of lie, and yet we all manage to survive, right? Everyone has to navigate a world of untruths, and some lies are bigger and harder to live with than others. But hey, the guy at the next cubicle has some dark secrets, too. People lie to the level at which they're comfortable, and everybody has a different threshold. This gets into some deep, dark psychology, but truly deceptive people just don't care as much about the truth as the rest of us. They even start believing their own stories, which gets us into the realm of the pathological. In the famous words of George Costanza, "It's not a lie if you believe it."

So what did Armstrong give up along the way? His integrity? Absolutely. His class? Yes. His reputation? Sure, at least for a while. Those are his sacrifices, though, and they could have little meaning to him. In the end, he got what he came for, and he will get it again. This is why people lie over and over again.

We all want winners and losers. More importantly, we want it to be easy to tell the difference between the two. But it's never that simple anymore, and maybe it never was. We want people to pay a steep price for deceiving us, but we're willing to forgive them as soon as they show the proper signs of contrition. We extract our pound of flesh and move on. It's the best and worst of us.

And it allows a former superhero who raced through the mountains and touched lives and healed wounds, all built on the foundation of a great lie, to live an incredibly comfortable life. And to live that life, perhaps, without a shred of guilt or remorse.

Lance is comfortable with that lie; so comfortable that he decided to tell the most naked truth this past year and discovered that nobody liked his answer. Maybe it's better to just lie every once in a while, just to give the people what they want. Allow them to hold on to a few chapters of the fairy tale. It's one way to become more popular. Instead, Lance told the truth—the truth we couldn't handle—and the backlash might have him considering a return to his old life.

You know the one. It's filled with private jets, willing sycophants, and unapologetic deception.

I DON'T CONDONE VIOLENCE,
**BUT IF ANYONE**
**EVER SAYS A GREAT**
**COLLEGE TEAM**
**COULD BEAT A POOR**
**PROFESSIONAL TEAM,**
PUNCH HIM IN THE FOREHEAD.

# DYSFUNCTION JUNCTION

**I** **CHECKED INTO THE CHIC HOTEL** on a frigid winter night in New York City with one thought in mind: sleep. Fighting a cold that made my head feel like it weighed fifty pounds, I took the key and headed to the elevator, ready to throw open the door to my room, unpack in less than two minutes, throw on some shorts and a baggy T-shirt, and crash.

Everything went smoothly until I opened the door and couldn't find the light switch.

I rubbed my hands along one wall and then the other, searching for any lever or button or slight depression or impression that might connect electrically to a lightbulb—any lightbulb. I was becoming a pathetic comedy skit, feeling up the walls in a pitch-black room like a mime. I rammed my foot into a wooden stand. At one point, I knocked over a small lamp and bumped some magazines off a table. I think I remember a knee bump into a swivel chair, too.

I felt like an incompetent—and loud—private investigator.

This went on for a while, until I wised up enough to wall-walk my way back across the room and reopen the hallway door to create more light. The moody and seductive hall lighting allowed me to find the frosted sliding bathroom door, and from there I'm not entirely sure if I eventually fell asleep naturally or knocked myself unconscious on an art deco–inspired hanging fruit basket.

Oh, and there was also the time in San Francisco when I came to the humbling conclusion that you've never felt truly old until you find yourself calling a woman in her twenties, wearing nothing at all—me, not her—to ask how to turn on a shower. It wasn't a short conversation, either—more like a remedial, step-by-excruciating-step instruction. She spoke slowly, overenunciating in a voice that was probably twenty or thirty decibels louder than her normal speaking voice. The whole thing had a convalescent-home feel to it.

I've never once claimed to be MacGyver, but for God's sake, all of you hotel-room designers, listen to me for a minute: Is it at all possible we could ramp up the functionality a little bit?

This trend is more prevalent and sillier on the coasts, where I presume the designers are engaged in some kind of endgame arms race in an effort to out-cool rival hotels. More fashionable faucets and slicker light fixtures are apparently the way you make your mark. In Miami, there was the hotel shower that was just too damned hip to have a curtain or a door. Instead, there was a glass wall that covered about a third of the space, which was a great feature if you wanted to water the carpet.

And how about the snazzy joint that had designer pillows that must have been chosen so they could double as disaster-prevention sandbags in case of an unexpected tsunami on the eleventh floor, high above the legendary Phoenix floodplain?

Somewhere along the line, hotel designers started creating rooms not for the customer but for other designers. I'm envisioning an annual convention where awards and bonuses are handed out for that bathroom faucet in Los Angeles that sent water splashing back at the mirror. The hotel executives in attendance probably rose as one to cheer the slide show that depicted the switch-less lamp in Austin that stumped me for three days. At this convention I'm imagining, anyone in attendance heard uttering—or even thinking—the word *user-friendly* earns a lifetime ban.

Oh, here's one other piece of advice for every high-end hotel chain: ditch the evening turn-down service. Unless you plan on tucking in my kids in order to allow me to kick it with my wife in the adjoining room, rest assured that I can figure out how to fold back the corner of my sheets all by myself. Providing, of course, that I can turn on a light and see it.

Listen up, you trendy sophisticates who know all thirteen different shades of orange, from burnt sienna to pumpkin: chill the fuck out. My knee is still bruised from that swivel chair, and my confidence is still shaken from that call about the shower.

I'm traveling, which means I'm exhausted, hungry, and dying for an on-off switch that announces itself for what it is.

So can you do a brother a solid for once? I'm not asking for much, really. You can keep your fancy swivel chairs and your medicine-ball pillows if you must. Just toss a little simplicity my way, when and where I need it most.

# PLAYING THE GAME
# OF YOUR LIFE

**L**ET ME SAY THIS UP FRONT: this is not a true story. It's not really even based on a true story. But please, allow me to fabricate a family for the purposes of our discussion. They will be a lovely group, I promise. Over time, I believe you will learn to admire them.

They're a hardworking family from Rochester, Minnesota. Mom is a respected schoolteacher in the local public school district, and Dad has a middle-management gig—you know, the kind kids aspire to reach when dreaming of a career.

They live a humble life, spend frugally, and make a very solid living on their combined incomes of $71,000. They have two sons, Kyle and Austin, who fell in love with football during adolescence. Austin, the younger of the two by just seventeen months, was good enough to earn a scholarship to play at Iowa

State University. Kyle was a better student but a worse football player—and, frankly, more responsible overall than Austin—and he did well academically at Texas Christian University. Kyle got into politics in college and saved enough money from his part-time job at Best Buy to spend two months as an intern on Capitol Hill after his sophomore year. He had big ideas and big dreams, and he was ready to explode out of college and change the world.

Austin's college football career unfolded in mostly unspectacular fashion. He made a poor first impression by getting into some trouble with his coaches for partying during his first month on campus. He was a marginal student who chased girls with more passion than he pursued either academics or ball carriers. But there was one quality Austin possessed that always superseded everything else: he was likable. People liked being around him, and perhaps because of that, things always seemed to work out for him. Sure enough, after college he landed a solid job working for a local businessman who remembered him from his high school playing days in Rochester.

Kyle, striver that he was, landed gainful employment right after college, too, a year earlier than Austin. His parents never worried about him the way they did Austin, and Kyle confirmed their faith by setting himself on a path to a solid future. He made slightly more than Austin, but their lives had changed drastically. Despite working three of his four years in college, Kyle graduated with massive amounts of college loan debt. His parents helped as much as they could, but TCU is expensive. It might not seem like much to a fifty-year-old with a long work history, but Kyle's monthly loan payment of $427 was a massive burden for a twenty-three-year-old. His job required some long road trips, so he bought a reliable car that set him back another $400 a month. Add in his $800 rent, and Kyle was lucky to save $250 every month.

He had always been shrewd with his money, but the dream of owning a home appeared hopeless. That $250 a month in savings didn't add up very fast in a strong economy with rapidly rising house prices.

Austin, of course, had no college debt. Not a penny. His football scholarship took care of everything, which allowed him to save far more than his brother. He and his girlfriend—the boss's daughter, natch—were able to save enough to buy a house together in Rochester in short order. Within eighteen months, they took advantage of the hot housing market to sell the house for a nice profit and buy a nicer, newer house in a better neighborhood and still pocket more than $3,000. Austin had ideas for that money—"play money," he called it—but his girlfriend urged him to do something responsible with it. And so, as he always did when responsibility was being forced upon him, he called Kyle for suggestions on what he should do. The older and more mature brother, no doubt thinking of his own situation, suggested he put the money in a 529 educational fund for down the road. When he hung up the phone, Kyle had a strange thought: for the first time, he envied his brother's life.

Austin had a new house with a cushy, stress-free gig he'd landed because of his football background. He had the beginnings of a college fund for his future child. And Kyle, frugal to the point of obsessive, couldn't manage to get out from under that college loan payment that mocked him on the fifteenth of every month. He was more responsible, smarter, and harder working than his brother, but none of that mattered on the fifteenth of every month. He began to think of all that debt as a giant, unscalable wall blocking his financial growth. He'd always dreamed of the day when he could get into the game of buying, fixing, and selling a house for a profit. He knew he had the savvy and skills to pull it off, but he couldn't get started without qualifying for that first house.

His brother, of all people, was in that game. Kyle wasn't close.

The story of Kyle and Austin plays out across America. The names, towns, and colleges change, but the basic truth doesn't. Some of you reading this will relate to Kyle's responsibility and earnestness. Others, even those of you who don't really care much for reading, will see yourself in the carefree, debt-free dude.

Millions of Americans share Kyle's burden. But when this very scenario is entered into the argument against college athletes being paid, something strange happens: the sports media shouts it down. The common refrain—college athletes get nothing for their labor—ignores the educational opportunities a guy like Austin gets from college, as well as the gift of exiting college debt free. This would not be possible without the ability to run and tackle, or dribble and dunk.

The long-term benefits of an athletic scholarship should not be minimized. It's hard to say this without being labeled a soulless shill for a corrupt and unjust system, but an athletic scholarship—on its own, without any of that other stuff around to cloud the picture—provides a sizable head start in life. If played wisely, that head start can give you a chance to lap the competition.

The enormous salaries commanded by college football and basketball coaches have helped trigger the rigorous discussion of compensating the athletes who play for them. In my opinion, the tipping point came when the University of Alabama's Nick Saban leveraged an offer from the University of Texas to get a raise from Alabama that jumped his annual salary above six or seven million dollars. It just felt ugly, and it fed the ugly juxtaposition of the rich, conniving white coach and the black players who struggle to pay for slices of pizza on Friday night before putting in the work to make the coach a hero on Saturday afternoon. I get it. It's uncomfortable.

But the same media members who rally for athletes to be paid keep forgetting about the *no-college-debt* thing and the generational boost it creates. Housing costs aren't going down, and the ability to get into the game early is an undeniable advantage. The financial benefits can set the table for the rest of your life. The country is filled with bright, capable young men and women from hardworking families who have college degrees and good jobs but can't get ahead because of those midmonth loan payments.

Think I'm overstating it? Okay, then consider the two-trillion dollar debt our government owes, and how some economists and politicians worry it could capsize our nation. Do you know that our national debt is only the second-biggest debt in this country? The first: college tuition debt.

And that part of this story is not fabricated.

We can argue over payments or salaries or stipends for college athletes. We can jostle over whether it's accurate to call a scholarship a "free education" when it comes with the onerous time demands an athlete faces and doesn't cover the entire cost of a student's matriculation. But what we shouldn't overlook is how much of an advantage it is to leave a university—often times, a university the athlete wouldn't have qualified to attend without being an athlete—with an unencumbered financial path in his sights.

Is it too much to ask, amid the howls for NCAA reform in the name of the starving and deprived college jock, that we also include a little grain of postcollege truth? No bills, great connections, and a society that falls all over itself to assist the former high school and college star.

Millions of other productive, responsible kids, many of whom never cared much for tackling other humans, could certainly give you an earful if you care to listen. You could start with Kyle.

YOU NEED TO
START LIVING LIFE.
IF YOU'RE SAVING
YOUR MONEY TO
GIVE TO YOUR KIDS
AS AN INHERITANCE,
YOU MIGHT AS WELL
SIGN THEM UP FOR
A COKE HABIT
RIGHT NOW.

# FOR PETE'S SAKE

**T**HE VOICE WAS MURKY AND DARK, the lyrics often indecipherable, but I was hooked the first time I heard Nirvana lead singer Kurt Cobain. His voice spoke to me in some indefinable way, a feeling that intensified when I discovered he was born twenty minutes from my childhood home and at one point worked at a restaurant less than a mile from my house.

The music press fell all over itself praising Cobain. He was described as an antidote to the superficial hair bands that preceded him. The adulation was rampant, and it cut across lines of class and culture. The *New York Times*, the *Village Voice*, *Rolling Stone* magazine—they all seemed to be in a competition to heap admiration upon Cobain and Nirvana.

One song in particular, "Smells Like Teen Spirit," captured the attention of the critics. It was called "the anthem of a generation," and it raced up several charts despite being virtually impossible to understand without a printout of the lyrics.

Those lyrics were considered meaningful and pained:

*With the lights out, it's less dangerous*
*Here we are now, entertain us*

Sounds deep, right? Cut right to the core of your being, don't they? But what if the critics were wrong? What if the words were not only far less meaningful than the critics believed but were, in fact, mostly meaningless?

Cobain himself changed his story on what the words meant. The band's drummer, Dave Grohl, once said, "Just seeing Kurt write lyrics to a song five minutes before we sing them—it's a little hard to believe the song has a lot to say about something."

Was Cobain putting words to the angst of a generation, or simply putting words to sounds?

Nirvana, like many bands—even great ones—often started with a melody and then sought words that fit it best. "You need syllables to fill up space," Grohl said. "You need something that rhymes."

Grohl is now the primary songwriter for the Foo Fighters. He had the closest access to Cobain and actually collaborated with him on "Smells Like Teen Spirit." It doesn't matter, though: Grohl's assessment of the randomness of Nirvana's lyrics is not the perceived and accepted view of the band. It has been overwhelmed and ignored, drowned out by the mythology surrounding Nirvana. Fantastic tales and inferred meaning have won the day.

This isn't an isolated example of myth overcoming a less fantastical reality. When respected and authoritative couriers—the nation's most powerful music critics, for example—deliver a message, that message has a way of becoming its own truth.

This is a routine occurrence in sports, especially the NFL, where authoritative and definitive voices extol the brilliance and transcendence of coaches who are masters at creating their own mythology. All of the praise takes on a life of its own, forgetting along the way that all of these legendary coaches didn't win anything until they found the right quarterback.

Bill Walsh, the hallowed creator of the West Coast offense, had a losing record with the San Francisco 49ers until Joe Montana became his starting quarterback in 1980 and touched off a period in which the 49ers won the Super Bowl three of the next seven seasons. Bill Belichick's genius was a slow build; he was 36-44—and fired—after five seasons as head coach of the Cleveland Browns. In 2000, his first year in New England, he started out 5-11 and was 0-2 the following season before Tom Brady became his starter and led the Pats to a Super Bowl win.

No coach in the NFL at this moment has more mythology swirling around him than Pete Carroll. He's a very good football coach, no doubt, but his status seems to have all the ingredients for the Legend Sundae: several scoops of misremembering with a healthy sprinkling of the downright unbelievable.

The appeal is undeniable. Carroll speaks like he coaches, in a frantic and ebullient fury. He attacks words, leaving little room for commas, periods, or the recipient's comprehension. It's an onslaught, really, and it can feel motivational even if the topic is as mundane as a grocery list. It's no wonder it plays well with the young athletes he coaches.

There is rarely a knockout line; instead, he jabs and feints frenetically with a belief system polished over thirty years and an energy level that would be admirable in a man half his age.

It would be hard to name a football coach over the past decade—in the non-Belichick, non-Saban division, anyway—who has been more adored than the Seattle Seahawks head coach. It started at the University of Southern California, where Carroll built a mini-dynasty from 2001 to 2009, and the media hoisted his reputation like a crane lifting a steel beam to the top of a skyscraper. A few floors were added after his Seahawks beat the Denver Broncos in Super Bowl XLVIII.

Carroll is more than a coach, and here's where his reputation gets a little tricky. He's a good story, and that good story—call it The One and Only Pete Carroll Story—has led to a syrupy and distorted perspective on his coaching legacy.

It's easier that way. It really is. It cuts down on the hate mail from fans and the discomfort around the team when you lather the current messiah with a thick and foamy layer of admiration. Maybe drop a small, gratuitous shot in your column to create the appearance of "fairness"—and to avoid being labeled a suck-up by your colleagues—and call it good.

It's not that Carroll isn't interesting or talented. Compared with the gloomy Tom Coughlin or the protective Jeff Fisher or the unimaginative Mike Smith, Carroll feels like a revolutionary, a New Age guru selling a cure-all potion. He has engineered quite a personal reinvention, that's for sure. More than a decade ago, in his late forties and coming off an ugly firing as head coach of the Patriots, Carroll was a debatable hire at USC. In fact, he was the school's third choice behind Dennis Erickson and Mike Bellotti. But whatever past failures—there was an unsuccessful stint as Jets head coach, too, in 1994—evaporated when Carroll got to Southern California. Maybe it was the beach or the weather or the welcoming spirit of Los Angeles, but Carroll sharpened his vision of what it means to be a coach. There's no doubt he found the messenger for his career repackaging when he teamed with Yogi Roth, a man who describes himself on his website as "adventure-preneur, storyteller, media personality, college football analyst, best-selling author, motivational speaker, coach, actor, and aspiring mapmaker." Carroll adopted Roth's "Life without Limits" philosophy, and the two appear together regularly at speaking engagements.

One BCS title and one Super Bowl championship later, Carroll is now minted as a football immortal. All fine, but it would help if everybody got a glimpse of how he got there. I'll be up front about this: there's no resentment or animosity motivating me to drop the anvil on Carroll's glossy resume. But would you think less of me if I perhaps noted a few—I don't know—discrepancies? Irregularities? Footnotes? Call them what you'd like, but they all have one thing in common: they've all been ignored.

The Pac-12 Conference, which was the Pac-10 during Carroll's USC run, has been as cyclical as any conference in the country. Good coaches build formidable staffs, put together a couple of good teams, and then are usually hired away. Even the most successful stories have a shelf life. The NFL is still the gold standard of football coaching, but losing a top coach is an accepted part of life, and good coordinators bolting for head-coaching jobs is as predictable as the tides.

And despite all that, despite the expected turnover and the accepted ups and downs, Pete's Pacific Coast run came at a time when the conference was at an all-time low. Washington, UCLA, Arizona State, and Stanford—all situated near attractive urban centers that should be magnets for recruits—spent the better part of Pete's decade in the netherworld between dreadful and rebuilding. Every conference relies on certain teams to carry on its traditions, and as Pete cut a swath through the Pac-10, its alpha-male programs were limp and lifeless. It's instructive to note that Cal, an institution where the academic side has often been at odds with the aims of the football program, was probably Pete's overriding concern during his best years.

The landscape on the West Coast allowed Carroll to parlay USC's brand as really the only fully committed football powerhouse west of Austin, to dominate recruiting. Unlike Big Ten and Southeastern Conference powers, the Trojans didn't have to share the four- and five-star talent. For the majority of the 2000s, they got all of it.

Carroll's roster was so stocked that Clay Matthews, later one of the NFL's top defensive players, couldn't even start regularly for USC. Don't misunderstand: Pete deserves praise for taking full advantage of the conference's weakness, and his reputation as one of the best recruiting closers is well deserved. But something happened during Carroll's last couple of years in Los Angeles that triggered a rampant case of national media amnesia.

Carroll's Kryptonite arrived in the form of two young and gifted coaches: Jim Harbaugh at Stanford and Chip Kelly at the University of Oregon. Within a short period of time, Carroll's Trojans were being embarrassed by both. Harbaugh, in fact, took a 40-point underdog—a *40-point* underdog—into the LA Coliseum and handed Carroll not only a shocking 24–23 loss but also a coaching clinic along the way. And then, two years later, in 2009, he destroyed USC 55–21, a beating so merciless that Carroll uttered the famous question "What's your deal?" as the two met at midfield after the game.

Since Pete asked, here's the deal: the conference and its coaching simply returned to its normal level, which meant that the advantage Carroll inherited evaporated. Pete's last regular-season college game was at home, against a forgettable University of Arizona squad, in front of a mostly empty Coliseum. USC lost.

Oh, and did I mention that Carroll hired a special-teams coach, a move not allowed under NCAA rules? It's a rule that's apparently understood by the 126 other Division I coaches, but not Carroll. There were other rules that weren't followed at USC, and the overall weight of Carroll's unwillingness to follow them resulted in a suffocating set of sanctions against the program.

No worries for Pete, though, because he didn't stick around to clean up the mess. He bailed and, in 2010, signed a massive contract in Seattle, where his first big move was to trade draft picks for career backup Charlie Whitehurst. That didn't work out, and neither did his decisions to acquire quarterbacks Tarvaris Jackson and Matt Flynn. After two years, Carroll's Seattle reign looked a lot like his previous two attempts to coach in the NFL: he was 14-16 and staring directly into the grim reality of heading into year three with his future in Flynn's hands.

While USC was dealing with the stink left in Carroll's wake, the Seahawks were being rebuilt by respected general manager John Schneider and Carroll. The men reshaped the roster, adding speed on both sides of the ball, but speed alone couldn't address the stark reality of a remarkably pedestrian offense.

And then, in the 2012 draft, the Seahawks rolled the dice and selected a young quarterback from the University of Wisconsin named Russell Wilson—a player they had already passed on twice. Only five foot eleven—several inches shorter than optimal quarterback height—he suddenly gave the Seahawks the ability to turn 5-point losses into 4-point wins with his brilliant instincts and quick feet. The offensive roster remained dotted with players who caused zero amount of jealousy throughout the league, but Wilson elevated the offense with the guile and maturity of a longtime veteran.

Seattle won a Super Bowl after the 2013 season, and Carroll's image was reborn. His boundless enthusiasm, good looks, and New Age coaching practices made him the football king of the moment. He's a gum-chomping, back-slapping, always-smiling guru of a new gridiron age. And none of it would have been possible if he hadn't attached himself to a quarterback who could drive his coach's image rehabilitation.

And then, in 2014–15, Carroll's Seahawks made it to another Super Bowl. They had the Patriots beaten, or so it seemed to everyone watching, until Carroll made perhaps the dumbest call in the history of sports. You know how it went: despite having Marshawn Lynch, the most bruising runner in the NFL, Carroll called for a pass play from the one-yard line with less than a minute remaining and New England hanging precariously to a 28–24 lead. Wilson threw an interception, and the entire country was silent for a split second before erupting in unison to ask the only question worth asking: What the hell was he thinking?

Maybe it shouldn't be surprising that Carroll outsmarted himself. Mythical heroes always seem to author their own undoing, and Lynch himself believes he didn't get the ball at the end of the game so that the NFL, and Carroll, wouldn't face the awkward scene of being forced to give the MVP trophy to a man who embarrassed the league with his season-long behavior toward the media. If Carroll based his play-calling on this scenario, it was a case of Pete trying to outmythologize the mythmakers, and it cost him and his team a championship.

At the highest level, football coaches are essentially talent accumulators, men who are ultimately successful only if they find the right guy for the most crucial position: quarterback. Bill Belichick's career record before Tom Brady: 41-55. Nick Saban in the NFL: a failure because he could not land a Pro Bowl–level player at the QB position during his two years with the Miami Dolphins, which produced a 15-17 record.

The prevailing narrative of Pete Carroll barely acknowledges this fact. It is routinely devoid of historical context or even any semblance of perspective. Instead, we get an endless stream of stories about Pete the soothsayer of personnel, Pete the master of finding talent in the late rounds, Pete the player's coach who elevates performance with relentlessness, mindfulness, positivity, and an audacious kung fu mind-set. He's a coaching wizard at both the college and pro levels; a man with a magical and unrivaled touch.

You know what disappears into the ether? Any proven faults—even any *possible* faults. He inherited a playoff team from Bill Parcells in New England and failed miserably. He presided over a meltdown at USC that started on the field and ended in the NCAA's version of a courtroom. He overdrafted in Seattle for offensive lineman James Carpenter and pass rusher Bruce Irvin, both in the first round. He gave away three picks for Percy Harvin, then essentially gave away Harvin after he punched two teammates. Those, apparently, are just inconvenient facts. So is the post–Super Bowl story of five Seahawks failing tests for Adderall, a stimulant banned by the NFL for players who don't have a valid prescription. And just as he did at USC, Carroll denied any knowledge of these drug-related issues. Pete knows all and sees all, the omniscient overlord, unless what he's supposed to know and supposed to see doesn't fit into the tidy story line.

I'm not looking to crucify Pete Carroll. I'm just looking for a little balance. You know, toss in a few uncomfortable realities alongside the breathless praise. I'm not holding out much hope, though. Nothing sticks to Teflon Pete, which is the way it always works for likable people with a truth to create and a story to tell.

# SOBERING TOPIC

**I** **DON'T PRETEND TO BE** an interior decorator, but for a room containing people addressing such a dark and serious topic, I would have guessed the motif could have been just a bit more uplifting. Maybe some star lilies in a vase? Some orchids perched on a countertop, perhaps? Anyone for some sheer linen window treatments to lighten things up some?

Instead, the walls of the Al-Anon meeting were gray and maroon. I was roughly ten years old, trailing a few feet behind my mom, already feeling the weight of a somber and intimidating moment. My mom was there to talk to the family support group about my dad's drinking problem. I don't even remember the meeting. In fact, it's possible they didn't allow me inside, but I distinctly remember the dark walls. They might as well have been bleeding on me.

We didn't talk much about this issue as a family, and why would we? My young life was a mixture of sports, friends, and motorbike riding around the coastal dunes of western Washington State. I knew about my dad's problem, but it wasn't mine. I was filling my days to the point where my life was hectic. After divorcing my dad, my mom married another alcoholic, who once got into a fistfight with his stepbrother in front of me on Thanksgiving. That ended with my stepdad rolling down the driveway. I remember the sound—fist landing on cheekbone—because of its violent *splat*, and also because it's hard to forget.

I have a certain level of respect, and fear, for alcohol and the nasty world overconsumption manages to create. I live by my own little gospel saying: "I like it so much I never drink too much."

It's a motto that was put to a severe test when I graduated from college and landed a baseball broadcasting gig in Las Vegas, hardly a dry county. I traveled with minor league players who pounded Budweiser at a remarkable rate. Listen, I'm serious about this. Don't just move on to the next sentence, because I need you to focus on four important words:

. . . *at a remarkable rate.*

I quickly learned that throwing down beers was a badge of honor in the sport. Young dudes, after a game in the desert heat, need a beer or nine to cool down. And that warm-up—call it the postgame pregame—happened before they left the yard. After that, they traveled to places like the Tap House or Four Kegs to vanquish the remaining suds in the city.

At the major league level, the stories are strikingly similar, with one difference: they include people and players you would recognize. Minor league drinking, just like hitting, prepares you for the next level, where the intensity increases.

In the early 1990s, the front office of one big league team decided it had a clubhouse drinking problem. (I'm going to be vague on the specifics, but trust me: this story is true.) There was a time, not that long ago, when big-league teams had big glass-front beverage refrigerators, the kind you'd find in a 7-Eleven, in the players-only dining room. The refrigerators all had at least two shelves stocked with cans of beer. On this particular team, players—and we're talking star players—would go straight from the dugout to the refrigerator at the end of every game. They'd grab four or five beers each, take them back to their lockers, and rehash the game with four or five other guys who were doing the same thing. Day game, night game, didn't matter. Games that ended before three o'clock in the afternoon were washed down with cans and cans of beer. Games that ended near midnight? Same deal. It was more collegial than nasty—just guys having a few after work—but it wasn't healthy, and it immediately turned potentially dangerous every time a player left the clubhouse and put the key in the ignition.

About midway through a lousy season, the general manager decided to do something about it. He knew he would face mutiny if he removed the beer from the clubhouse altogether, so he came up with a different solution: he replaced the refrigerator with a keg. His goal was to reduce the drinking by making the players get up and walk back to the food room and refill their cup every time they wanted a beer. He figured they'd bring one back to their locker, maybe head back for one refill, and then decide to shower and head home before everybody was blowing a 0.18.

The first day of the clubhouse keg came on the first day of a home stand. The players walked into the clubhouse, saw the keg, and immediately went berserk. Honestly, they would have been less upset if they'd found their jerseys in tatters and the catcher's gear hung in effigy. They couldn't believe the gall of the GM. But for one night, the ploy seemed to work. After the game, the players took their cups, refilled them a time or two and went on their way.

The next day, a Wednesday, happened to be a day game, which meant less time to come up with a workaround for the GM's dastardly move. But if you learn one thing from this story, it should be this: never underestimate a ballplayer's ingenuity when it comes to maximizing his postgame alcohol consumption. Because that morning, about three hours before game time, one of the team's most prominent players sauntered into the clubhouse holding six beer pitchers high above his head, like a conquering hero. His buddies in the corner actually cheered. He handed out one pitcher each to four of his friends and kept two for himself. And that, ladies 'n' gentlemen, is how the Great Big-League Keg War was won.

Baseball seems pretty well suited to drinking, right? There

isn't that much sustained physical activity, and, unlike in other professional sports, players are fed in the clubhouse after games. (In basketball and football, players leave the locker room and head for a nice restaurant. Not in baseball, where the postgame meal is a ritual.) And even though the mentality has changed considerably over the past two decades, with players becoming far more health conscious, alcohol remains woven into the fabric of the game.

And that's why it's even more astonishing when an athlete in the NBA or National Hockey League, sports where cardio strength is vital, can remain productive while treating his liver like his worst enemy. Dennis Rodman is perhaps the most famous example. He could stay out all night, alternating shots of Jägermeister and tequila, and be the most active and crazily heroic player on the court twelve hours later. Rodman's drinking exploits were perhaps unsurpassed in the annals of professional sports, save for maybe those of Babe Ruth, and anybody who had the misfortune of watching *The Celebrity Apprentice* could see the toll it took on both his brain and his body. In the offseason, Rodman would stay out at clubs until past closing time—often buying drinks for everyone at the place—go home and sleep for two, maybe three hours, and then get in his Ferrari and drive around the greater Los Angeles area with no real destination in mind. After a couple of hours of that, he'd park and walk into a health club—one of which he was not a member, incidentally—and proceed to spend an hour on the StairMaster at the highest speed. Most people, having had that much to drink the night before, would have still been passed out. Somehow, his body just worked differently.

Matt Barnaby, a former NHL right wing with a wicked sense of humor that helped him land a job as a broadcaster after his fourteen-year playing career ended, told me that alcohol at times felt like a coping agent. He was tough but not physically imposing, and he said the mental aspect of the game weighed on him—especially heading into a night when he knew he would have to face an opposing enforcer thirty pounds heavier and several inches taller. Barnaby told me a few stories one day as I peppered him for behind-the-scenes NHL tales. I had him cornered off air in an ESPN studio, and there was one question I had to ask:

"What about the legendary stories of vodka consumption among Russian hockey players?"

"All true," he said with a laugh. "All true."

I'm sure it couldn't have been any more shocking than an experience I had with a minor league manager. I had been tasked to bring him a file on player statistics after a game one time, and when I entered his office, the first thing I saw on his desk was a carafe of wine. Before you shrug, understand something: this wasn't one of those slender, dainty, let-the-*Château-Pétrus*-breathe carafes you might see in an upscale restaurant. No, the skipper's carafe was more like a vase for a sturdy plant, like a rhododendron or maybe a peach tree. It was filled to the brim with a (probably cheap) cabernet.

After handing him the papers, I thought I'd make a little

small talk and ask who might be joining him. I was met with an icy stare and complete silence; the wine was his and his alone. I left the room wondering if a bison could finish that much wine without running into a fence. Later I was told that this carafe was filled and drained nightly, never accompanied by a meal.

I learned my lesson after a while. I stopped going out with the minor leaguers because of the fear welling up from my childhood. I was fully aware of what alcohol could do to a person. I don't want my kids shuffling into one of those gray-and-maroon rooms, a step or two behind their mother, even if the place had decided to add a few orchids.

# MEMO TO COACHES:
## DID YOU EVER IMPROVE
# AT ANYTHING
# WHEN SOMEBODY
# YELLED AT YOU?

# THE SOUTHERN ILLUSION

**Y**OU HEAR COMMENTATORS AND COACHES and executives say it all the time:

Nothing is permanent but change.

Everyone nods listlessly at this banal half-truth. Yep, the sports world is in constant flux: offensive lines change, owners change—even Kobe Bryant's shot selection changes occasionally—and there's a reason for that. If it didn't, it wouldn't be something that exists in the actual world.

But I have to say there is one grand constant in the world of sports: fan paranoia.

There's nothing more durable than the skeptical and conspiratorial who see devious machinations at work behind even the most innocent happenings. And there's nothing harder to kill than the assumption that any dynasty in any sport in any region is the result of a powerful, sinister force that creates and controls the variables that allow the dynasty to exist and flourish.

Superior intelligence? Nah. Smart scouting? Please. Determined recruiting or shrewd management? Hell, no. Stocky men wearing dark glasses and whispering in public—*those* are the guys who make it happen. They've got motives and secrets. It's like the Watergate scandal: follow the money.

When ESPN created the SEC Network, which broadcasts football, baseball, basketball, and other sports featuring Southeastern Conference schools, something broke loose inside the sports-paranoia industrial complex. From the day of the announcement, any positive comment about the conference was viewed as commercially driven propaganda. What else are they gonna say, right? It was not only money driven but also targeted specifically to minimize the conferences with which ESPN has no television contract.

It didn't matter that ESPN has a contract with every league not named the NHL. It didn't matter that CBS has been viewed as "the Home of the SEC" for more than a decade. It didn't matter that ESPN broadcasters, me included, had heaped praise on the SEC long before the SEC Network was a twinkle in President John Skipper's eye.

It was the perfect storm. The combination of SEC football dominance, the inaugural year of the wholly subjective college football playoff, and the launch of the SEC Network created a category 5 storm of sports insecurity. The conference had won eight of nine national titles, produced the most first-round picks, and posted the best bowl record over a ten-year stretch. But none of that mattered.

The SEC was going to dominate because ESPN said so. The scheme to promote SEC dominance was hatched in a room (underground bunker?) at ESPN headquarters in Bristol, Connecticut. It didn't matter that precisely zero of the twelve members of the playoff committee had ever been employed by us. It didn't matter that each of the committee members was uniquely successful and qualified, completely unlikely to risk personal integrity and a lifetime reputation just to see Georgia make the playoff over Oregon or TCU.

I decided to investigate. I called the three most well-connected agents to get an inside view of the process. These three represent nearly every one of the fifty highest-paid college coaches, working behind the scenes to navigate the ins and outs—and false leads—of the NCAA's byzantine structure. They work the same hallways, competing for clients, but they don't always agree. There is one point of agreement, though: the South, from its fans to its boosters to its university administrators, views the sport differently.

My conversations with them made it clear why the South feels so empowered by its football. Obviously, the mind-set could be viewed as an indictment of the region by many, but instead of directing animosity or jealousy at the SEC—and those who are presumed to be paid to praise it—perhaps a small dose of understanding would prove beneficial.

Here's a sampling of what the agents said:

"USC may be the best job when you rank them," one said. "You can lock down LA and get almost all the great players from around there, but on a Saturday at three o'clock, there's a lot of things to do in Los Angeles. Football isn't as important. In Alabama, the state shuts down at that time. It's their entertainment. It just means more to them."

Said another, "What else is there to do in those small towns?"

Would you trade that year-round boredom for a more rabid fan base and a better football team?

There are times when statistics laid bare can be harsh, even cruel, but that doesn't make them any less accurate. Of the four regions in the United States, the South ranks lowest in education levels, and the lowest-ranked states—Louisiana, Mississippi, Arkansas, and Alabama—reside squarely in the SEC footprint. Those states, in turn, produce a large number of athletes who may not qualify academically at many Pac-12 or Atlantic Coast Conference schools.

Those academic hurdles can be cleared far easier in the South, where only one SEC school, Vanderbilt, regularly makes the *U.S. News & World Report*'s rankings of the top one hundred universities. The ACC, in contrast, had six in the most recent rankings, while six SEC universities fell below one hundred.

One of my agent friends said, "Where many universities, like Michigan or UCLA, want to win at football, they want to keep up the appearance that it's not more important than academics. Not in the SEC. Alabama likes that Nick Saban is the highest-paid coach in the sport. That makes them feel important. It's a source of pride."

Or, in other words, many Alabamans, undoubtedly aware of their national image as less than erudite, overcompensate through football. This kind of mind-set would be viewed as unbalanced—"misguided priorities" would be the proper term— in the Northeast and West. These are universities first, right?

Would you trade even a small part of your academic integrity to win more football games?

Poverty is a troubling national issue, with income disparity front and center, but its intensity and impact are even greater in the South. According to the US Department of Agriculture, which tracks poverty, every red state from New Mexico to South Carolina has higher poverty rates than the national average. One in four children in the South live in poverty, according to the Children's Defense Fund. Those dire economic situations create mental and physical stresses that extend far beyond money problems. On the other side, deprivation can create a singular drive to escape those circumstances. Fear is a powerful motivator, and one SEC assistant coach told me it plays a major role in the southern game.

"Kids from Florida and Georgia are hungrier than California kids," he said. This was not a revelation to him, nor did he think it should be for anyone else. He gave his opinion nonchalantly, as if every coach understands this essential fact. He felt that football in these places had reached an exalted status, viewed by many high school stars as the only option for a better life.

Would you trade that all-or-nothing, desperate mentality for a better local football team?

Is it outrageous to suggest that the SEC's football dominance was born of negative outside factors? In the give-and-take of everyday life, is it possible that widespread poverty, a failing educational system, and colleges willing to make academic concessions in exchange for athletic glory helped to create a football-mad region? Is this how these small towns—towns with inferiority complexes rooted in history—wound up being the centers of the college football universe?

I can see the southern football fan wincing now. I can feel the sting. I can predict the anger. But take solace, southern football fan: the pain and confusion you're feeling is exactly what all those ACC and Big Ten schools are likely to feel when they line up against your boys from September through January. And that's when you can stand and shout and puff up your chest, and tell the rest of the world it's worth it.

# WALL OF SHAME

**L**ET'S JUST GO AHEAD and call this the worst theory ever:

A physicist at Temple University, probably a brilliant young man with a good family and a solid moral compass, woke up one morning on the wrong side of common sense. Rongjia Tao came up with an idea to thwart the devastation wrought by tornadoes in the Plains states, and his idea was this: build several thousand-foot tall walls across the central United States to block or slow the progress of these storms.

And you thought the Wildcat offense was a gimmick.

Tao's idea—remember, the man is a scientist with years of academic and practical work behind him—was shot down quickly by every meteorologist worth his barometer, in addition to any child over six years old.

Storms producing tornadoes can rise eleven miles above the

earth's surface. Using a thousand-foot wall to fight one would be the equivalent of using a roll of paper towels to mop up a tanker spill.

This idea came from a highly educated man. He thought about it, let it stir around in his head for a few weeks, maybe jotted down a few numbers on paper, and presented it to the world, completely oblivious to how it would be viewed or dissected.

Seriously: *Giant walls to stop tornadoes?* I can see everyone from North Texas to southern Minnesota pleading with his or her local planning commission: "Can you please, *please* put the thousand-foot wall in *my* neighborhood?" I mean, think of how property values would skyrocket with the addition of a wall as tall as the Chrysler Building. Once these walls prove to be a success, maybe they could be followed by manufacturing papier-mâché cars to lessen the impact of traffic accidents, or rubber commercial jetliners that bounce to safety after hitting a mountain.

How could this happen? It's an idea so bat-shit bananas that even a B-list actor playing a fumbling scientist in a D-list comedy about stopping tornadoes—a movie that would bomb now, but come to think of it, might have had a chance with Jerry Lewis in the sixties—would stop before announcing his theory to the civilized world.

Rongjia Tao's ideas were published in a paper titled "Eliminating the Major Tornado Threat in Tornado Alley," in the *International Journal of Modern Physics*. It was peer-reviewed, which meant other scientists had to read it before it was accepted for publication. Well, I've got a theory of my own: Tao's peers, in this case at least, weren't the kind who possessed strong, dissenting voices.

Crazy ideas take shape and build momentum only when nobody steps up and offers a serious rebuttal. Or when the person holding the crazy idea isn't willing to surround him or herself with challenging, independent thinkers.

In a weird way, Tao's idea seems downright practical when it's compared with some of the more outlandish decisions made in the sports world.

Let me lob a few your way:

- The University of Notre Dame once hired a high school coach, Gerry Faust, to run its football program.

- Former NBA commissioner David Stern once introduced a new ball for the league without consulting the employees who would actually use it. You know those guys; they're called *players*.

- The Minnesota Timberwolves once drafted point guards back-to-back—as in, one after the other—in the first round of the draft.

- The NFL commissioner, franchise owners, and team doctors spent a decade refusing to listen (and often suppressing) evidence proving that repeated shots to the head could lead to depression, dementia, and sui-

cide. Thirty years later? Billions of dollars in settle-
ments and potential lawsuits.

- A University of Kentucky basketball coach once sent a
recruit thousands of dollars in cash through the mail.

- The Oakland Raiders twice hired head coaches who
had never been head coaches—not even at the high
school level.

- The Los Angeles Clippers' draft picks from 1985 to
2010, with the notable exception of Danny Manning.

- The New York Jets. Just . . . the New York Jets. All of
them, and all of it.

Suddenly, in light of that list, the tornado wall doesn't feel
like such an isolated bolt of lunacy.

Is it possible—and hear me out on this one—that at least
some of these misguided, foolish, half-cocked sports decisions
could have been avoided if teams and leagues (this might be a
little rough, fellas) just hired more women?

Prisons are filled with men, and for a very good reason. We
are more aggressive, and that testosterone-fueled intensity
might have benefits on the field, but it creates impulses and
hubris that lead many, many men down the road to poor
judgment. This is not a phenomenon limited to less-educated
men—far from it.

From presidents and senators, to sports commissioners and Wall Street CEOs, to school principals and priests—look, don't take my word for it: watch the six o'clock news tonight. It might as well begin every night with the anchor looking earnestly into the camera and saying, "Good evening, and welcome to the latest dumb shit some men decided to do." Followed, of course, by four minutes of weather and some sports scores.

Women are smart—really smart. New research from Daniel and Susan Voyer at Canada's University of New Brunswick, a meta-analysis of almost 370 studies, found that girls earn higher grades than boys in every single subject, including math and science. This proved true of every country studied.

Women can handle the heavy lifting: an overview of hedge funds over a ten-year period, as reported by the *Wall Street Journal* in August 2014, showed that funds with women in decision-making roles and a higher percentage of women in senior leadership positions provided better returns than funds with a more male-dominated hierarchy.

Women make us safer. National crime statistics furnished by the FBI show that married men are far less likely to commit a crime than single men are, no doubt owing to a wife's ability to convince her husband that robbing that convenience store or stabbing that police officer is, in general, a really bad idea.

Do you sense a pattern here? It's subtle, so pay attention, lean in, and work with me to connect the dots.

Ah, you see it now, don't you? Nailed it.

Women make us smarter when they're in the room. We lose

some ego and gain some empathy. We lose some control, too, but we gain some perspective once we're forced to see a world outside the dude huddle. And while we might not like to admit it, it's statistically proven that when men join with women, the collective IQ goes up.

Look around at male-dominated industries: sports, the military, financial institutions. What do you notice? For one thing, a series of regular meltdowns and crises that could have been avoided if prevailing male attitudes had been diluted by the qualities women bring to a situation.

Sometimes the sports world's unwillingness to embrace capable women rises to the level of sheer lunacy.

Legendary Florida State University football coach Bobby Bowden once said the following:

"As a Christian, conservative man, I would vote for Condoleezza Rice for president if she ran."

And in response to the news that Condoleezza Rice—the same one, because there's only one—would be a member of the committee to decide college football's Final Four, Bobby Bowden said the following:

"She's never even played the game."

Think about that for a moment.

The same person Bowden sees as capable of holding the highest office in the most influential country in the world, a country with the most powerful military and the largest economy in the galaxy, *can't be trusted with deciphering whether TCU is better than Michigan State.*

As secretary of state during George W. Bush's second term, Rice negotiated with dictators. She navigated the chaotic world of international diplomacy. She worked at the highest level in an administration that was waging two wars half a world away.

But hey, we'd better not let her near our football! She never laced 'em up, so how can she judge the efficiency of Mississippi State's offense?

Bowden isn't alone. He sees it the way most men in sports see it. I guess I should qualify that: they see as much as they can from behind those walls they keep hoping are going to protect them from tornadoes.

# FIFA IS SO CORRUPT THAT YOU WONDER IF THEY HAVE A HEADQUARTERS OR JUST A SECRET HIDEOUT.

# HEAVY WEARS THE CROWN

**D**O WE HAVE ANY IDEA—any idea at all—just how much better the very best are? It's easy to state blithely that someone or some team is the best, but that's much different from analyzing and understanding what it takes to become an all-time great.

We don't have to bother with any of that, of course. We can rationalize our defeats, blame those lousy referees, and think of our careers as just a series of bad breaks orchestrated by resentful bosses. It's probably tougher for men to concede the idea of someone else's greatness, since we do exactly what society does: judge our personal standing on our professional accomplishments.

So it's hard, right? It might be the hardest thing to do: take a big gulp of pride and acknowledge that the best aren't just sort of better but exponentially more talented. And not only that, but also they face one burden the rest of us—the common, the average, and the regular—never do.

The best are always targets. The best players, teams, managers, coaches—it simply can't be overstated how much of a target they are. The best inspire the best. Muhammad Ali got everyone's best fight. Kobe Bryant gets everyone's best defensive effort. Bill Belichick gets every coach's best game plan. Peyton Manning gets every defensive coordinator's most complicated rush scheme *and* every defensive end's most focused and violent drive off the edge.

Let's start by taking a closer look at Kobe, who seems like the perfect test case for our theory. For the fifteen years of his prime, Kobe faced stacked defenses, designed specifically to stop him, every single night. His opponents, clearly motivated, got a better night's sleep the night before and watched a little more film the next morning. Stopping Kobe could change a career, establish a reputation, make a guy some money. And it wasn't just players, either; coaches put in more preparation time for Bryant, and yet he would still routinely drop thirty on them. What would Kobe have averaged if those teams had put an average, unmotivated defender on him? What if coaches didn't create defenses specifically and solely designed to slow the inevitable onslaught? What if opposing coaches started their pregame meeting by saying, "Okay, we're going to let Kobe get his and worry about everyone else"? Is it outrageous to speculate that he could have approached 50 points a night?

This concept isn't reserved for sports. Competitive, driven

people do their best to rise to meet a challenge. Through the years, I've noticed a change in myself whenever I have a special guest planned for my show. For instance, the two times that President Obama came on the show, I spent considerably more time preparing and thinking about what questions I should ask. Former NBA commissioner David Stern and Dallas Mavericks owner Mark Cuban earned extra attention, too, because I know if I'm not at my best with those people in the room or on the phone, I'll get devoured.

One night in Portland, Oregon, on an ornate stage in a concert hall nicknamed "the Schnitz," I watched in awe as Jerry Seinfeld brilliantly undressed a heckler during his stand-up routine. He was a master. In fact, Seinfeld's ad-libbing on the building's architecture was far more entertaining than any part of the well-crafted performances of two headliners I'd seen a month earlier in Las Vegas. Seinfeld was quick to point out that his Portland stop was the first or second performance of his tour, so he was airing new material. Even with the one or two jokes that fell flat, it was obvious from the beginning that his deadpan delivery and hilarious give-and-take with the audience was significantly better than the well-cooked and overly practiced material of other comedians.

Greatness is just . . . different, is all. After the New England Patriots defeated Seattle in Super Bowl XLIX, Peter King of *Sports Illustrated*'s Monday Morning Quarterback column sat down for an extended interview with Tom Brady. It was a rare and illuminating view into the mind of Patriots coach Bill

Belichick. Noticing something on tape that would have gone undetected by nearly every other coach, Belichick preached patience and north-south running for his backs and receivers after catching passes. The reason was obvious to Belichick, even if it wasn't to anyone else: the fast and aggressive Seahawks defense earned its accolades with a unique form of gang tackling. The Seahawks were such sure tacklers that the first defenders on the scene would take care of the ball carrier while the next guys to arrive would attempt to strip the ball. It was well orchestrated and extremely well executed. So in the two weeks before the Super Bowl, any Patriot who caught a ball in practice was instructed to turn up the field immediately, with the idea of being content with four- and five-yard gains instead of attempting to pursue bigger gains. The strategy worked perfectly, as Seattle's dominant defense was exhausted and frustrated by the fourth quarter. Contrast that with how the Denver Broncos, coached by John Fox, were frustrated and overwhelmed by the Seahawks' tactics in the Super Bowl the year before.

Sometimes, greatness means paying attention to the little things. Those little things, it seems, often turn into big things.

Former Patriots offensive lineman Damien Woody once described Belichick's practices to me as more intellectual exercises than physical. "You would practice things all season," he said. "Little things and situational things that you would probably never use. It didn't make sense to me at first. Then, in week thirteen, the situation would come up, and you would say, 'Ah, wow, this guy is different.' We were never surprised on the field in New England. We always felt more prepared."

The best of the best have a different mind-set. Think for a moment about how sensationally gifted Red Sox ace Pedro Martinez was in his prime. Everything was stacked against him. He played his home games in Fenway Park, a hitter's paradise, and pitched during an era of artificially induced offensive production not seen before or since. He pitched most of his career in the American League East, which meant that he pitched a lot of games in Yankee Stadium, another hitter-friendly park. And yet Martinez was virtually unhittable for the better part of a decade. He threw four one-hitters—that most frustrating of achievements—struck out seventeen against the 1999 World Series champion Yankees in one of those one-hitters, and rarely had a bad start. His numbers were amazing, but how much better would they have been in a pitcher-friendly park like the Oakland Coliseum, home of the most foul ground in the big leagues? (Fenway has the least.) What if Martinez had pitched most of his career in a less-ominous division, like the AL Central or in the DH-less National League?

Leonardo DiCaprio has never starred in a stinker. Is that because he's the luckiest actor in Hollywood, or could it be that his talent and range are accompanied by some of the better instincts of anyone in the business? Is it by chance that DreamWorks Studios went an entire decade without a single animated flop, or that the Beatles never whiffed on an album? Those who are supremely gifted are working on an entirely different level.

They're not just lucky, and they're not just benefiting from advantages not afforded to the rest of us.

In fact, the gap is greater than any of us would care to admit.

The 1995–96 Chicago Bulls are perhaps the best example of team greatness. They won a regular-season record seventy-two games, losing just ten, a record that is even more remarkable when you consider the rigors of the NBA schedule. As impressive as that was, though, the true measure of their greatness could be found in the first games of each playoff series—including the NBA Finals.

Historically, the winner of game one has a big edge in a series, and coach Phil Jackson's Bulls certainly knew that. The first game sends a message and sets a tone. Whatever happens in that first game is likely to seep into subsequent games. It stands to reason that both teams elevate their focus and desire at the beginning of a playoff series.

During their 1996 playoff run, facing the best teams the league had to offer, Chicago won the first game of each series by an average of 17 points. After a rock-star regular season, Michael Jordan, Scottie Pippen, Dennis Rodman, and company went into the playoffs as the biggest targets in the history of the league, and they won game one by a margin that was four times higher than the average. That kind of sheer dominance happens only when a team possesses a roster-wide determination to be mentally and physically prepared every single night.

Peyton Manning is the Kobe of the NFL, a one-man version of the 1995–96 Chicago Bulls. What's better than beating Manning? Pretty much nothing, by the looks of it. Manning has had some rough playoff games, sure, but can we reserve a moment to reflect on the fourteen years he spent with the Indianapolis Colts in the American Football Conference East and South, where every defensive coordinator in his division got two cracks at him each year and defensive coordinators had so much tape on him they could have gone full Errol Morris on him anytime they wanted? What happened over those fifteen highly scrutinized years? The quarterback sliced up division rivals, often humiliating them regardless of the linemen who blocked for him or the receivers who caught his passes. He was a step ahead of every defensive trick devised by every defensive coordinator whose professional worth depended on his ability to confound Manning.

Greatness is the ultimate humbler. It's born of so many things that it's difficult to know where to start. It's DNA and drive, sure, but it's also intellect and instinct. It's being humbled early and obsessed late, and it's so rarely in our presence that we should embrace it rather than resent it.

Yes, that's right. We should succumb to our better natures and concede the obvious: greatness is rare, and precious, and those who possess it should be appreciated, as much as that might hurt.

# "WRONG GUY, YOU'RE ON THE AIR"

**E**VER HOSTED A PARTY, and the only people who showed up were the ones you hesitated to invite in the first place?

Welcome to my job.

I've never suggested that talking about sports rises to the level of astronaut or cancer researcher when it comes to importance to society. And I completely understand that my job is several notches below sanitation inspector in terms of public safety. I'm not delusional; I know my dance partners at the societal soiree are probably editorial cartoonists and wine critics. It's a fun gig, and I won't apologize for it, but it's always best if we take care of the important stuff—bridge building, national security, sewer maintenance—before we get to the business of arguing about point guards or the NFL draft.

As with any business, there's an unspoken downside. The

smart thing for me to do is to keep the biggest pain in the butt to myself, since I have it better than most and complaining could hurt business.

But today, on these very pages—actually, on this page right now—I'm breaking down that barrier. I'm going boldly where none have gone before, barging blindly into that dark world that separates good business from good sense.

In sports radio, most migraines begin with "the 1 percent."

(Or at least used to, but I'm getting ahead of myself.)

You see, radio research indicates that only 1 percent of listeners ever email or call a show. Now, it's important that I delineate the demographic of this 1 percent. It's not the thoughtful and articulate teacher who gave me a compliment at the grocery store. It's not the quirky, funny chef who buys me the first round because he says I make his prep go faster. It's not the businessman who downloads my podcast because he's too busy for regular radio but says he appreciates that I make him think.

No, those aren't the people who call a show—any show. The ones who do, the ones who are willing to remain on hold for forty minutes before stumbling through a painful eighteen seconds of mostly incoherent but intense conviction, are lonely. They're sitting at home using a landline phone—I picture a shoulder cradle—in the midafternoon. They tell their friends they talk sports regularly with radio hosts but fail to tell them the host is thirteen hundred miles and eight states away.

I have a name for these folks. I call them, collectively, Wrong Guy.

Wrong Guy thought Tim Tebow was the next Brett Favre. He thought LeBron would never win a title. He was vehement in his belief that the NFL should never change its rules to protect players from concussions. He still contends steroids didn't help power hitters, and he initially sided with Ray Rice's beating of his fiancée and tried to convince me—before the videotape made the position impossible—that she started the whole thing. He also has an unnatural inclination to swear that every marginal white college basketball player will be the next Kobe Bryant. Oh, how he wants that to happen.

Wrong Guy tends to dominate sports radio for one very obvious reason: Right Guy is busy with family and professional responsibilities. He's busy preparing to manage a client or create a new partnership. Or maybe he's looking forward to the simple pleasure of having a peaceful lunch with another human being. Right Guy just doesn't have the time or the interest to expend energy trying to win an argument over which college football conference is best or which third baseman would be the best fit for the Yankees in a post-A-Rod world.

And I can make the case that this 1 percent issue is universal. This guy is everywhere.

New York City is the financial, fashion, media, and cultural hub of North America. Over the course of dozens of trips there, I've had memorable dinners and thought-provoking discussions with everyone from bartenders and cops to sales executives and commodity brokers. Each one of these people is informed and ready to engage in meaningful dialogue.

And yet, if you happen to turn on WFAN Radio, one of the nation's first all-sports stations, you'll hear callers who sound like retrograde Al Bundy with a side of pure, undiluted delusion. They're straight out of central casting, bringing their thick New York accents and the confidence of an industry titan—despite the fact that most of these guys work jobs that require name tags.

Wrong Guy does not ask permission. "I've got four points here, guys—hear me out." Wrong Guy does not traffic in gray areas. He often ends his tirade with "It's so obvious," after explaining how every sports league is run by the Mob.

How is any of this possible? Are all the Wrong Guys stored in a Staten Island warehouse with a phone bank and a refrigerator full of Red Bull and bile? They're actors, right? It's got to be a comedy troupe funded by the station.

The most fascinating aspect of this, at least to me, is the durability. Wrong Guy makes Cal Ripken Jr. look like the thirty-year-old slacker riding his skateboard around town wondering where he left his medical marijuana card. Despite being mocked, lectured, and humiliated day after day by host after host, he never leaves. Wrong Guy is the cockroach of sports. You can't kill him off. He'll be back tomorrow, at the same time with his same provincial sports opinion, ready to convince you he sees an angle nobody else can spot.

I used to cringe when Wrong Guy called. Then I started to notice something.

As off target as his shots might be, and as knee-jerk reactionary as he undoubtedly is, Wrong Guy is telling you how the average guy in the average bar on the average street corner is feeling.

That was the first thing I noticed, but not the most important.

When I sifted through the anger and the noise, it became clear that these guys were having an impact on how some teams were making decisions. The phenomenon was most obvious in the loudest and largest media markets, like New York.

Prior to the 2010 baseball season, the Mets, forever in the shadow of the Yankees, acquired pull-hitting, slow-footed out-fielder Jason Bay after several Yankees free-agent signings. Mets fans—including all the Wrong Guys—had been in an up-roar over their team's inability to add anything interesting to the roster. They repeatedly blasted Mets executives on local radio and spoke of rooting for their hated crosstown rivals, if for no other reason than to support a more aggressive franchise.

Bay was a horrible fit in the cavernous outfield of Citi Field, and no baseball executive—not even, I believe, those with the Mets—thought his acquisition made sense for this team despite averaging 30 home runs and 95 RBIs over the previous six sea-sons in Pittsburgh and Boston. As a Met, he was a disaster from the first home stand. And yet it served its purpose. It quelled the mob momentarily.

Thirty years ago, before the explosion of sports radio, the voice of the fan could be found in irregular letters to the editor of the local sports section. These would generally appear on Sunday before vanishing for another week. Now, though, it's a twenty-four-hour blitz of personal attacks, vicious second-guessing, and snarky venom aimed at coaches, owners, and general managers. As they found their voices, fans began to name names.

Team owners are listening—not only listening but also feeling the pressure exerted by consumers who demand answers. Executives ignore the noise at their own risk; pretending it doesn't exist comes off as disengaged and uninterested in the concerns of their customers. Two decades ago, they could hide, but now they're drawn into the fray.

Take a look around sports right now and notice how fast a little bit of choppy water can turn into a tsunami. See how precious little time new coaches and their staffs get to turn around a sagging franchise?

It wasn't always this way. Coaches used to be able to impose a three- or even a five-year plan before a judgment was rendered. What's changed?

The pressure, that's what, and it's ignited at least partly by large and vocal fan bases. Their platform, increasingly, comes in the form of the local sports radio stations. It certainly doesn't come from newspapers, which have lost so much relevance that the very idea of a letter to the sports editor seems like a relic from the days of manual typewriters. Fans have no platform on local television, where sportscasters get two minutes to speed-read the highlights. The single biggest megaphone—bigger than Twitter and any other social media—is sports radio, where disgruntled fans line up for the morning show and bang the drum well into the night.

In smaller to medium-sized cities, the teams still have some leverage over public opinion. They can deny access to media and Bigfoot opposing views; single-sport towns or those with fewer options generally prefer a more supportive media.

In the big cities, though, the competition among the media is far more fierce, and the guys doing the competing have bigger salaries at stake. In places like Philadelphia, Boston, Chicago, San Francisco, Detroit, New York, and Los Angeles, there are two or three newspapers, five local television affiliates, and two or three sports radio options, with each of them looking to rise above the others by whatever means necessary. How do you do that? You do that with stronger opinions and by digging deeper to break stories—mostly negative stories.

The media landscape has not only changed but also widened, with teams getting wise to the benefits of controlling both message and messenger. Teams in larger cities with mega–cable television partners are making deals with star players not because they help on the field or bring good character to the locker room but because they're assets for continued viability among fans and advertisers.

Kobe Bryant, coming off a torn Achilles tendon, signed a monstrous two-year deal with the Lakers in a move that was viewed by NBA insiders as a parting gift to Kobe for his years of meritorious service. What other rationale could there be? The deal clearly shredded the team's salary cap and delayed a much-needed rebuilding process. I asked Jeanie Buss, the team's co-owner, why they did it. She didn't deny that Bryant's status as the franchise's trophy wife was attractive to their local broadcast partner, Time Warner Cable.

In other words, it was a blatant and unapologetic move by a large-market franchise to put popularity over building a superior product.

New York has glamour, history, and financial advantages. Look at the city's current roster of eight professional franchises and ask yourself this question: How are so many of them so bad? It defies logic.

I see a common theme: reactionary owners and front offices that are all too willing to allow the desires of fans to dictate their transactions. The Knicks' late-season trade for Carmelo Anthony in 2011 made emotional sense—Carmelo's East Coast heritage and star power being unquestioned. However, he has deteriorated physically, can't deliver wins, and owns a contract that will be an anchor for years. But that trade was promoted and applauded by the media and a whole city of Wrong Guys for months before and after it happened. The same thing happened when Brett Favre came to the Jets for the 2008 season, and when Michael Vick came to the Jets six years later. All three of those moves—Anthony, Favre, Vick—began with virtual election campaigns on radio and in the newspapers. Eventually owners James Dolan (Knicks) and Woody Johnson (Jets) pushed for them to happen.

Philadelphia works in reverse of New York. With some of the angriest and most unhinged radio callers in the country, and a media that feeds off them, the folks in Philly push people out of town, not in. They led the push to dispatch Flyers general manager Bobby Clarke in 1990, and the franchise has never been the same. In 2012 the crazed fans and media also demanded a new football coach, even though Andy Reid had delivered five NFC title game appearances in eleven years, and the conjoined twins got their wish.

The five largest cities in the country have thirty-six pro franchises that produced just three champions in 2013–14: Los Angeles Kings, Chicago Blackhawks, San Francisco Giants. Two of those are NHL franchises, which means that they get the least attention from the media and therefore feel the least amount of outside pressure. In an era when star athletes are nearly pathological about their desire to increase their profiles and further their brands, doesn't it make sense that large markets would dominate the landscape? Or, at the very least, shouldn't they be more competitive?

The biggest liars in the world are politicians, of course, but owners, general managers, and coaches of major sports teams come in a close second, for one reason: they claim they never listen to sports radio. Oh, they hear it all right. Sometimes indirectly, but they hear it loud and clear. And what they hear can sometimes turn out to be detrimental to their franchises.

The unruly and unwashed mob of the 1 percenters remains almost always wrong, but they've embedded themselves into an interesting slot in our sports culture. They're annoying but heard, misguided but influential. They finally have a platform, and they're going to use the hell out of it.

The standards for print and television are relatively high. Radio, though, is just short of a street-corner fistfight. Dysfunction and absurdity move the needle and are thereby heartily encouraged. Facts are optional, and outrageous narratives can build momentum and take on lives of their own over the course of an eight-minute segment. Nobody ever said that the smartest and most thoughtful people—on the topic of anything, really— have the most impact. Loud, reactionary and sometimes just plain crazy can garner attention and gain traction from owners deeply concerned with keeping fans happy.

Sports radio has given the 1 percenter an invitation he's never had to a party he's decided to dominate. There's Wrong Guy over there holding court. He showed up early and plans to stay late. He's got this theory about sports and the Mob he's sure you'll love to hear.

# I CAN'T RELATE
## TO SILLY PLAYERS.
## HOW MANY GREAT PLAYERS
## HAD A NICKNAME
## THAT STARTED WITH "SWAGGY"?
## DO YOU THINK
## TIM DUNCAN EVER
## REFERRED TO HIMSELF
## AS "SWAGGY T"?

# A TAXING MATTER

**T**HE HOW-TO MANUAL ON PARENTING got misplaced long ago at our house. So, like most dads, I'm pretty much winging it, making up profound life lessons as I go along. For the most part, I try to dispense the kind of commonsense wisdom you can't get from anyone else. My top three: be kind, have manners, and don't run into traffic.

My fourteen-year-old daughter, Olivia, raised my parenting expectations to an unrealistic level. Smart, generous, and organized, she's like sending Tom Brady out for your opening drive. Anything that could go wrong probably won't. She's fourteen going on forty.

My son? He's a whole different ballgame. He's eight going on hazardous weather. He's the parenting equivalent of riding a malfunctioning roller coaster in a dust storm. He's endlessly sweet and bright, yes, but those qualities are combined with a worldview that can generously be described as beyond oblivious.

Consider: He once wore his favorite shirt inside out at camp. For a week.

He views playing in the rain his weekly quota for showering.

What's a father to do? For one thing, you pick your spots. Too much big-picture advice gets lost in a haze of greasy hair and inside-out shirts. But as it turns out, I was presented with a prime teaching moment several years ago while we were vacationing at Disney World. And make no mistake, I seized on that bad boy like LeBron attacking an alley-oop on a fast break.

Here's the backstory: one day at lunch, Jackson began complaining that the service was a little on the slow side. On its face, no big deal, right? Pretty innocuous. It's not breaking news for a hungry boy to want his food *now*, but he doubled down by adding that—in his reasoned estimation—the lines were a little longer on the rides, too.

This was my cue to begin dispensing wisdom. (It's like I'm a jukebox and Jackson a quarter.) I had to remind the little guy that his dad was an employee of Disney (which owns ESPN), and because of that, those rides he'd been enjoying so much over the past few days were free. When you get hundreds of thousands of discounts that the general public doesn't, I continued, the proper and respectful course of action is to express your gratitude and to praise the Great Mickey at every opportunity.

That's a solid rule for life, right? When you're benefiting from a freebie or a discount, try to keep your misery to a dull roar. Turn down the volume a notch. Your life may be fraught with minor imperfections, but in the big picture, it's a safe bet that others have worse issues than coping with slightly longer than usual lines during a free trip to Disney World. So, young man, grumble to yourself.

I felt pretty good about this bit of wise parenting. I gave myself an internal high five and thought that someday Jackson would hark back to that day and marvel at the old sage who raised him.

My message to my son is the same one that I would convey to the Big 47 Percent. Remember them? They torpedoed the presidential candidacy of Republican Mitt Romney in 2012 when he was videotaped referencing the percentage of the electorate that doesn't currently pay federal taxes.

First off, let me say I'm down with any tax system that allows the poor and less fortunate to retain more of their income to elevate their and their families' lives. It should also be noted, however, that current tax codes in America are written to benefit businesses, not individuals.

Here's a nebulous term for you: *business expense*. It's the loophole of all loopholes, big enough to drive a thousand big rigs through. Cars, trips, dinners—whatever you got, it can be written off as a business expense. And let's just say that many, or maybe most, or—the hell with it, I mean absolutely *all*—small businesses find ways to—what's the word I'm looking for?—*manipulate* those expenses. It might not be $27,000-shower-curtain-for-business-use deceptive, and it might not be she's-a-call-girl-on-the-side-but-really-she's-just-a-valuable-member-of-my-hospitality-staff deceptive, but when it comes to write-offs, there are angles to exploit.

We also live in a country where the people who build the entire infrastructure, from roads to bridges to shopping malls, have jobs that take physical tolls that shorten lives. People who do the jobs most of us would never want—or simply couldn't do—deserve certain tax, educational, and insurance benefits that guys like me, a yodeler who rants into a microphone about sports, should never be offered.

But here's where the train jumps the track. If at any point in your life you are paying nothing while benefiting from those who pay a lot, could you keep your misery to a dull roar? Could you at least not be the flag-waving, gun-toting *leader* of the rich-guys-don't-pay-enough-taxes cavalry?

According to several reports, somewhere between 82 percent and 92 percent of taxes are paid by those wealthy, no-good folks who spend their days trying to figure out how to write off hookers and ski trips to the Swiss Alps. Oh, but wait: let's dig a little deeper into the lives of these so-called wealthy folks. It looks like the truth might be a little less exciting than you think.

Wealth, in fact, is so relative and geographically inconsistent that we don't really even know how to categorize it.

No reasonable person would argue that a $200,000-a-year salary in New York means the same as it does in Ames, Iowa. In other words, who is rich, and how do we decide? Many of those people who, on paper, might be considered rich might be dealing with the same check-to-check monthly grind as the 47 per-centers.

Say you're budgeting for a family in Northern California, where real estate prices are outrageous, gas is more expensive, school tuition can be daunting, and state and local taxes are higher than almost anywhere in the country. Your supposedly rich salary—combined salaries, more likely—of $158,000 can wither away like so many drought-ridden suburban lawns. Believe it or not, these *rich* people—no doubt yacht-and-vineyard-owning—are wincing as they write out the mortgage payment at the beginning of every month. It goes without saying that they don't own either a yacht or a vineyard, and probably don't know anyone who does.

But you—you rich $158k-per-year tycoon—are lumped into the same group of people that *does* own a fleet of whatever rich people have fleets of.

So it's easy to see how you—while raising three kids who will never appear on a reality show or a police blotter, while giving generously to local charities and schools (schools your kids share with people from every socioeconomic class), while building a family on the same rock-solid principles as the most upstanding of the 47 percenters—might get a little pissed off if you're being barked at by people who have been afforded the same life opportunities but just made poorer choices.

In other words, not everyone being labeled rich is remotely close to that. And not everybody with a zero tax burden is either a parasite or a victim of an unfair system. So is it okay for the most vocal of the 47 percenters to drop the bullhorn for a few moments every election cycle?

If you and a friend went hiking and he asked you to carry his backpack after tweaking his shoulder, you'd probably comply. He's your friend, this is a shared experience—hey, help your fellow man, and it might create a stronger bond between the two of you. But I'm guessing that you wouldn't appreciate it if you reached the summit and he turned to you and said, "You know what pissed me off? You didn't do your fair share of the work."

If your income doesn't rise to the level of taxable income, I feel you. I'm sympathetic and supportive of you making the most of what you have. I can and will argue that your children should have educational benefits that can make their futures brighter and more fulfilling.

But since my tax burden is paying for a chunk of that, can we make a deal? Can you at least have the self-awareness to realize that your shirt is inside out?

# WORLD CUP
# RUNNETH OVER

**T**HEY CALL IT A BUSINESS DISRUPTION, and the taxi
industry was primed to take one right between the eyes. What
happens is this: an industry becomes complacent, no competitors
in sight, and it ends up becoming vulnerable to transformative
change. And so, in the taxi business, Uber jumped in to seize a
new space in an old business model.

Uber created a digital taxi company with convenient rides
across town with a simple click and go. You can see them on
your mobile device—ratings, location, make and model of
the car—and within seconds or minutes, it's pulling up at
the curb. What's not to like about a business that lets you
be a more informed consumer? Uber now has a valuation of
$40 billion.

Technology has accelerated the pace of business disruptions.

What Uber did to the taxi business, Amazon did to retail shopping, and Netflix did to the video-rental business.

In sports, the World Cup is Uber to the Olympics' taxi business.

The World Cup is Mardi Gras with a ball. It's profitable for cities and television networks. It's an endless party for fans, and it's relatively simple to put together. You don't need to build luge tracks and ski jumps and downhill ski runs that will never be used again. The biggest upset of the 2014 Sochi Winter Olympics came weeks afterward, when NBC reported that it made a slight profit on the event. I guess even taxi companies get lucky every once in a while.

The financially disastrous 1976 Summer Olympics in Montreal were thought to be the death knell for the Olympic business model. But thanks to business executive Peter Ueberroth, who headed the Los Angeles Olympic Organizing Committee, the 1984 Summer Olympics—the first to have an official candy bar—figured out how to combine patriotism with entrepreneurial magic to make a few bucks. The boycotting Soviets helped launch the "U-S-A! U-S-A!" phenomenon, but hey—whatever it takes. Since then, though, everything has changed. The International Olympic Committee no longer seeks stunning and vibrant destinations to give the folks at home the proper visuals. Now it's money, and money alone, that determines sites.

Attention-seeking and warmongering Russian president Vladimir Putin, a man the Pentagon claims is driven to extreme control partly by Asperger syndrome, outspent and outpromised other countries to land the Sochi Olympics. An ugly and isolated coastal shithole on the Black Sea, Sochi slapped up a few living quarters for athletes and media and proceeded to produce the most forgettable Olympics since the last one. I can't remember one fucking thing that happened, but I do remember how hard NBC worked to find anything even remotely scenic to show on its patented panoramas. The network kept coming back to that one shot of that one mountain that wouldn't merit even a second look in Lake Tahoe or Park City.

The best event I ever attended was Wimbledon, hands down. With its cheeky British fans and its almost comical civility, it's in a class of its own. A big boxing match is second, based on its unbearable intensity and borderline vulgarity. A great boxing match in the 1980s was a cross between a violent car wreck and the best sex you ever had.

The Olympics is the worst, and there's no second place. It's the most bloated, overrated, difficult-to-cover event I have experienced in more than twenty years in the media. Most of the time—if you're lucky—there are a half dozen memorable events from any one Olympic site. As a reporter, your chances of attending the right event and witnessing the moment are infinitesimally small.

The television viewer at home never quite gets the scope of the Olympics. He can see those seminal moments over and over, followed by sharp after-the-fact analysis that makes everything feel organized and tidy. Many times, though, Olympic events are spread over hundreds of miles. You can spend hours waiting in line for a shuttle to drop off twenty-three different parties be-fore you step off to attend the finals of the biathlon, which—for the record—you can't even see while it's taking place.

The World Cup also necessitates being away from your fam-ily for three weeks, but the very nature of the sport creates a beautiful collage of spirit, food, diversity, and intensity. Heated rivals shake hands and exchange jerseys after games. Wins by poorer countries can transform a nation's self-worth. Losses are felt for months.

Cable sports networks are desperate for programming, and the World Cup has emerged as a singular gem. Any network with assets is dying to win the rights to televise it, and for good reason: you win, and you're making a sizable profit from Day One. America's growing Hispanic population increases its ap-peal. It's the perfect three-week espresso shot for our divided at-tention. Quick, passionate, intense—it's everything you could ask for.

The Olympics? Different story. It's increasingly obvious that NBC, based on its excellent coverage and strong branding through the years, is the only network interested in paying for it. The Winter Games, with predominantly white athletes from northern countries, feels as irrelevant and outdated as a rotary phone hanging in the kitchen.

They should adopt a new slogan:

The Olympics: When You're Nostalgic for the Cold War.

Uber. Amazon. Netflix. And now the World Cup. They're the future, at least until the next disruption.

WHEN YOU PLAY WITH LEBRON,
YOU HAVE TO REALIZE
**HE IS THE SUN.**
YOU'RE JUST A PLANET
**AROUND HIM—MAYBE**
YOU CAN BE THE MOON.
**BEST-CASE SCENARIO,**
YOU'RE SATURN
**AND GET SOME RINGS.**

# HATE THE PLAYER?
# NAH, JUST HIS GAME

**Z**ACH **LAVINE EXPLODED** from the Barclays Center floor and threw down a swooping, one-handed, between-the-legs dunk with such ease and grace that still photographs the next day made him appear to be hanging and posing—in midair—in the split second before he jammed it home.

And yet LaVine, with all that athletic ability, is not one of the first people mentioned when casual NBA fans cite their favorite players. Admittedly still a kid, he had averaged 3 points per game in the six games leading up to his breakout performance in the slam dunk contest in Brooklyn. He plays for the Minnesota Timberwolves, a team with all sorts of young former college stars: Andrew Wiggins, Anthony Bennett, Shabazz Muhammad. All this talent, in addition to the oft-injured but valuable point guard Ricky Rubio, resulted in the worst record (17-65) in the league in 2015.

Which goes to show: the difference between collegiate stardom and professional success is so wide, and so rare, that the statistics seem manufactured for the sole purpose of discouraging dreams.

According to the NFL, more than 66,000 athletes play college football each year, and just 300 of them will ever make an NFL roster. Do the math on that one. And of those 300, just 65 percent of them—195—will still be active after three years in the league. The hard truth is, by the time most players hit twenty-five, the NFL has no economic use for them anymore.

In basketball, guys like Jimmer Fredette, Pearl Washington, and Harold Miner not only tore up college basketball but also became mythical figures by the time they were twenty years old. They were can't-miss guys who missed badly, unable to crack an NBA starting lineup or, in Miner's case, stick on a roster.

That's reason number one I lost no sleep when Michael Sam, the first openly gay professional football player, was quickly and unceremoniously bounced from the NFL without appearing in a single regular-season game; the St. Louis Rams cut him at the end of the 2014 training camp, and he was signed and waived from the Dallas Cowboys' taxi squad midway through the season.

Sure, I have no doubt that the NFL employs its share of homophobes among players, coaches, and front offices. This isn't Hollywood or Comedy Central; it's a business that's not only all male but loudly all male. It's a place where educated, discerning voices can be drowned out by twenty guys grunting and another five gnawing on a locker room couch.

But when it comes to Michael Sam, can we let the voice of reason cut through all the irrelevant static?

The notoriously liberal Bill Maher used a few moments of his HBO show, *Real Time*, to point out the harsh reality of social change when he defended a young NFL player named Don Jones, who went on Twitter to display homophobic tendencies after Sam kissed his boyfriend live on national television during the NFL draft. The scene shouldn't have been shocking, but—given the context—it took over the nation for two weeks.

"The culture war is over," Maher said. "We won. But it was so unnecessary for so many to type what a jerk Don Jones was. Give the kid a minute to get enlightened. Remember how stupid you were at twenty-four? Now add football."

It's laughable for anyone to expect football to lead the way on an issue that states—and even the president—have struggled to fully comprehend. Progressive states such as California have battled over the issue of gay marriage, and yet the NFL was supposed to be the place where homophobia dies and everyone lives in blissful harmony? Maybe in a fairy-tale world.

And yet the media couldn't hide their contempt for the league when it came to the response to Michael Sam's coming-out and nationally televised display of public affection for his boyfriend. Of course Sam would make some players uncomfortable, and most of those players would understand—years later, probably—how silly it had all been. But football seasons are months-long slogs, and there's no time for a weeklong symposium on how to deconstruct what your parents or buddies may have told you about gay people. And it's probably not the NFL's job to dig in and decipher what the Bible says or doesn't say about a person's sexuality.

Athletes struggle with social change the way cities struggle with budgets. In other words, all the time. Hell, players called the commissioner the devil for changing rules on head-to-head contact. The inevitable emergence of an openly gay NFL player was always going to be awkward and unpredictable—for the player, the teams, and the media—and Sam's ordeal certainly lived up to that billing. The horrible hazing that so many predicted never happened, however, and the claims that Sam would be a distraction were preposterous and overblown.

But here's something that wasn't:

Michael Sam was never going to be an NFL player of note.

Go back to those forbidding survival numbers in the NFL. Read them again and place Sam in his proper context. His initial combine performance was perhaps the worst and least explosive I've ever seen from a supposedly top defensive player. He was terrible in space, a real killer in an evolving league that demands it from its linebackers. From the start, his skill set made playing linebacker a nearly impossible task. Even at the University of Missouri, he was more of a situational star. He rushed the passer well but was considered the second- or third-best defensive lineman on his own team.

But something happened after his senior season that ignited the media and set the stage for the craziness that followed:

Michael Sam was named SEC co–defensive player of the year.

It was mentioned repeatedly on draft day, as Sam fell and fell and fell, all the way to the seventh and final round. It was mentioned when he was placed on the St. Louis Rams' practice squad. It was mentioned when he was cut by the Rams and signed, briefly, to the Dallas Cowboys' practice squad.

It became the media's final word on any argument; proof of his ability to not only play but also star in the NFL.

He was judged on an award. An *award*.

"Of *course* he's good enough for the NFL," went the collective wail. "He was the best defensive player in the best conference in college football."

It shouldn't be necessary to point out the faulty logic here, but it is. Sam's NFL bona fides were based on past SEC Defensive Players of the Year. The last *X* number of SEC Defensive Players of the Year played in the NFL; therefore Michael Sam should play in the NFL. Otherwise it's discrimination.

Using the same logic, Michael Sam should be the NFL's Defensive Player of the Year, make All-Pro seven years in a row, and lead the NFL in tackles on his way to a Hall of Fame career. After all, that's what linebacker Patrick Willis of the San Francisco 49ers did, and he was the SEC Defensive Player of the Year in 2007. Stands to reason, right?

Let me ask you something: Is the NFL also anti-Christian? Because Tim Tebow was not only all-SEC twice while at the

University of Florida but also dominated the conference for two years as an inspirational and physical force unrivaled in the South. He then won several NFL games as a starting quarterback for the Denver Broncos, and then—in what should have been the prime of his career—couldn't even get a tryout with Jacksonville at a time when Josh McCown and Blaine Gabbert were given repeated chances.

What happened to Tebow was the same thing that happened to Sam. It's really pretty fundamental. Neither had the skill set that translates to the professional game. Neither did Pervis Ellison, Joe Smith, or Adam Morrison, all of whom were more profoundly dominant as college basketball players than Sam was on the football field.

This is nothing new. In the early 1990s, Dave Hoffmann was arguably the Pac-10's best linebacker at the University of Washington. He was a tackling machine, and that impressed NFL personnel people just enough to get him drafted in the sixth round of the 1993 draft. Erick Anderson not only led the University of Michigan in tackles for four straight years from 1988 through 1991 but also is the only linebacker in school history to win the Dick Butkus Award as the nation's best linebacker, in 1991. He was also co–Big Ten Player of the Year as a senior.

Like Sam, Anderson was drafted in the seventh round. He would start only one game in the NFL, as a fill-in for an injured Kansas City Chiefs teammate, and was jettisoned from the league for not having the requisite skills to play the game at the highest level.

Anderson never kissed anyone, of either gender, on national television. If memory serves, he didn't push a minicupcake into his companion's face during the same telecast. And let's not ignore that elephant over there: those moments—the kiss and the cupcake—did Sam no favors in what was essentially a job interview situation. They were startling to almost all players and fans, regardless of tolerance level, and to deny that is to ignore the obvious. Some players in the all-male, all-macho, all-young, not-all-enlightened world of professional football were undoubtedly uncomfortable with what they were watching.

So now that we've got both feet firmly planted in reality, let's stay there.

Dude was a marginal and situational NFL player at best, and he backed it up with an embarrassing combine performance. When you remove the ancillary issues, it's really not that difficult. He won an award in college, though, and it allowed the conspiracy theorists a convenient touchstone whenever the facts didn't fit the narrative. And that award, like the Heisman Trophy, has absolutely no correlation to an NFL future.

Go look at those NFL numbers again. Next, run your eyes down that Timberwolves roster. Lastly, revisit the football career of Erick Anderson, and then, as Bill Maher might say, add a kiss.

# RAVENOUS

**W**HEN I TOLD TALK-SHOW LEGEND Larry King that I regularly talk to myself—frequently while in the car, more frequently while jogging—he gave me a stricken look that made me wonder if the words that left my mouth were vastly different from the ones I intended. Wait, did I say I just knocked off a convenience store? No, Larry, I said I talk to myself.

Don't look so shocked. Millions of Americans talk to themselves. Studies show it's a sign of intelligence, so take that, Mr. I've-Interviewed-Every-Important-Person-in-the-Last-Half-Century.

Who can really say why we do the things we do?

Can you come up with a rational explanation for why you bought that ChapStick you didn't really need—the one that was positioned strategically next to the cashier? They call it an impulse buy, and it's supposed to explain why you pull into Dunkin' Donuts for a coffee when you're still hopped up from the last one.

You find yourself drinking a coffee almost reflexively, probably from a complicated formula involving strong branding, rising barometric pressure, some Ted Nugent lyrics, and the Illuminati controlling your mind.

You subconsciously feel like drinking coffee and—whoa!—suddenly your car just veered into a parking space next to a tall sign bearing a huge, steaming Styrofoam cup of coffee. Life is temporarily better.

We all do things that make no sense. When people ask why, we just shrug and hope the conversation moves on before we have to face the roots of our weirdness. We have no problem justifying our actions in our heads; it's all those people who are judging us who have the problem.

Irrational, inexplicable behavior is a big part of being a sports fan, and there's no better example than the fan who cheers athletes who have been guilty of committing despicable acts. In February 2014 Baltimore Ravens running back Ray Rice struck his fiancée—now his wife—so violently in the elevator of an Atlantic City casino that he knocked her out cold. When the elevator door opened, he dragged her out like she was a bag of topsoil.

You know the rest of the story: He was suspended for just two games, the outcry was swift and furious, and then the videotape emerged on TMZ showing the actual punch, and the Ravens were shamed into releasing Rice.

A few days after Rice was given his two-game suspension, Ravens fans cheered wholeheartedly an image of Rice at a practice. Even after the video evidence emerged, some fans wore Rice's number 27 jersey to a Ravens game. A group of them posed for a photo and posted it on social media.

Do these fans, mostly males, support domestic violence? Their defiant poses and smiling faces in that photograph could lead you directly to that conclusion, but I doubt that's the case. I think they would be outraged if a man—even Ray Rice—struck their sister, wife, mother, or daughter. But in their minds, they undoubtedly justified their support for a star player who had been publicly and deservedly thrashed.

This odd backlash is something I find personally offensive, but it's also something I've come to expect in sports. The minute fans pay money to enter an arena or stadium, they alter their standards for socially acceptable behavior. They are now rooting for the performer, whom they feel is an extension of them, and nothing else matters.

The phenomenon is widespread, cutting through geographic and socioeconomic lines. Portland, Oregon, is a city filled with civic-minded and overwhelmingly well-intentioned people. They recycle and ride their bikes and compost. And yet, during a multiyear stretch of Trail Blazers basketball, the team's likability level hovered between "Not at all" and "Slightly less than that." Even on days when aberrant player behavior was splashed on the front page of the *Oregonian* newspaper and polls showed a visceral dislike for the players on the roster, everything changed when the games began. Scorn and disdain were replaced by devotion and cheers.

Good people supporting bad, often criminal, behavior.

It makes zero sense.

The only plausible explanation I can offer is this: we all view sports as escapism. Deep down, paying for a ticket is paying for a performance. We don't care if Russell Crowe throws a phone at a hotel employee or a rock star trashes his suite at the Ritz-Carlton. We don't care that our favorite linebacker has four kids from three different girlfriends and supports none of them.

We pay, and they deliver. It's a straightforward transaction. The last thing we want to do is mess with their heads by booing them or judging them when they're playing at home. They'll get enough of that on the road, and we don't want to run the risk of disabling their next act with our disapproval. What's it hurt to give that sociopathic power forward—the one with a penchant for brandishing a tire iron—a little home cooking?

Consider sports as a little minicruise, with the ship waiting offshore to take us away from the weekly grind. When our team wins, it somehow elevates our lives, too. Studies show we feel better about ourselves when our local teams win.

Does that make our values lopsided and unhealthy? Does it speak poorly to the collective IQ of those who enjoy the games?

I don't think so.

Doesn't the art snob feel better about his place in the world when a new museum opens in his area code? Doesn't the foodie revel in the new bistro that just opened down the street? Isn't that how we judge ourselves against the next town over?

We're complicated creatures. You can't explain with any level of specificity what makes people tick, and what ticks them off. How can a decent father and husband cheer a man he would view with outright contempt if he weren't wearing his team's jersey?

It used to really bother me. I used to spend time trying to figure it out, to understand the psychology behind irrational fan behavior.

Now I just tell myself—yes, out loud—that you simply can't explain some of the things people do.

And then I pull my car off the road. Anyone up for a coffee?

# LIGHTNING
## WAS THE MOVIES
## FOR CAVEMEN.

# MEN'S WEARHOUSE

**B**RUCE BOCHY WAS MEMORABLE long before he began winning World Series rings as the manager of the San Francisco Giants. To call him a large man would be an understatement; almost an insult. His neck and hands are incredibly thick, his head legendary. He seems entirely capable of carrying large wooden beams, the kind used to build Alpine lodges, on his shoulders—cross-country. Even his eyebrows have a physical presence.

On a minor league flight to Colorado Springs in 1988, Bochy sat directly in front of me, talking to Padres prospect Shawn Abner. I was the play-by-play announcer for the Las Vegas Stars, and Bochy was finishing his playing career as a backup minor-league catcher. He and Abner, then a twenty-two-year-old who was in the process of going from phenom to bust, were talking about something called Rotisserie baseball, a concept that seemed abstract at the time. And not only abstract but quite possibly weird. Two professional baseball men breaking down which Montreal Expo would better serve their imaginary batting lineups was even less interesting to me than the two older women next to me bragging about their grandkids.

As it turns out, Bochy—now universally respected for his baseball instincts—was onto something back then. He was at the forefront of the fantasy sports industry.

More than forty-one million people in North America play fantasy sports. Roughly half of them are married, and nearly 80 percent of them hold a college degree. But here's the demographic nugget I want you to remember: 80 percent are men.

Dudes dominate sports gambling at an even higher rate. R. J. Bell of the betting site Pregame.com told me that roughly 97 percent of sports gamblers are men. The sports ticket market, buyers and sellers, is also overwhelmingly male. Of course, you already know that 100 percent of NFL and college football players are also men.

The truth about sports is not only statistical but also cultural. Every sport and nearly every business tied to it is largely a guys' playground. Not totally, of course, but awfully close to it. Name a vocation or avocation pertaining to sports—coaching, managing, scouting, covering, training, or gambling—and you can't go wrong assuming the practitioner is male.

Slowly, like a snail inching across a sidewalk, this is changing. Frankly, that's a good thing. More voices and perspectives originating outside the man tunnel are needed. Case in point: the

NFL's meltdown over domestic violence. This plague would have been limited—or maybe even prevented—if there had been women in Commissioner Roger Goodell's hierarchy with the standing to voice their concerns over the league's handling of what became the biggest sports story of 2014.

The male-dominated tyranny in the sports world has far-reaching repercussions. There's something bigger at work here: the normal discourse has devolved into a series of schoolyard arguments. On social media, especially Twitter, the conversation has become tiring and utterly predictable. Baseless accusations and hair-trigger condemnations rule the day. Self-righteous vitriol has overtaken analysis, and thoughtful discussion is nowhere to be found. Civility—the very thing the keyboard screamers are professing to defend—has been vaporized.

As a prime example, I present the outrage that stemmed from an article that appeared in *Men's Health* magazine in October 2014. The offense? The author had the sheer audacity to suggest that women don't view sports, especially football, the same way men do. "She sees the game differently than you," the subhead read. "Here's how, and what to do about it." The story was accompanied by a photo of a young woman, dressed casually but not suggestively, holding a red foam finger.

The story, written by a woman (incidentally) in a magazine targeting men, in no way discouraged women from watching sports, betting on them, or playing them. It simply reported empirical data indicating that fewer women's lives revolve around sports. Is there a human alive who would argue that central thesis? The piece went on to say that women would be more inclined to take an active interest in sports if the men in their lives spent less time analyzing on-base percentage and WHIP (walks plus hits divided by innings pitched, for the uninitiated) and more time discussing the personalities of the athletes. It never said that women were incapable of understanding Jim Harbaugh's jumbo sets or Pete Carroll's blitzing schemes. It merely reported that women connect with sports more viscerally when the athletes are humanized. For women, in other words, it's more about the center fielder's shoe collection than his average with runners in scoring position.

The late, great sports television producer Roone Arledge might have been the first to put this into practice. His "Up Close and Personal" vignettes from the Olympics were the linchpin of some of the most successful sports coverage in history. His belief that knowing the athlete's backstory, and not just his two-hundred-meter time, would keep the casual fan glued to his seat is the stuff of TV legend. Long after Arledge left the scene, the Olympics continue to deliver strong ratings among female viewers.

And yet, despite the unassailable truth of the *Men's Health* article, the magazine quickly pulled it. The social media outrage escalated to the point where the editors felt they had no choice. Detractors were out of their minds, claiming that the story rose to some heretofore-unseen level of vile bigotry and/or incomprehensible gender insensitivity. The indignation fed upon itself, eventually becoming a fetid mudslide that covered everything in its path. It got to the point where no-body would have been shocked if the assigning editor had been placed in witness protection, at least for the remainder of the decade.

The next morning on my show, I not only defended the magazine's right to publish the article but also decided to conduct an unscientific experiment of my own. I sent my producer's wife to the grocery store with specific instructions to examine the women's magazines carefully—and, you might say, cynically—positioned at the checkstands. What were the headlines? What were these women's magazines promoting? How were they targeting *their* primary demographic?

Here's a sampling of headlines from magazines such as *Cosmopolitan*, *Redbook*, and *Elle*:

"30 All-Time Greatest Songs to Masturbate To,"

"11 Hair Problems All Latinas Understand,"

"19 Date Outfits You Must Never Forget,"

"Perfect Fall Recipes," and

"Body Glitter Tips."

Well. What do you know? Do you think any of those would ever appear on the front of a men's magazine? I think I speak for men everywhere when I stand on my moral high horse and ask, "How *dare* they cater to their core female consumers?" Don't they know there are plenty of guys who would like to learn how to make a tasty October split pea and ham? Those damned *Cosmo* sexists.

Those magazine headlines illustrate what every sentient being already knows: men and women *do* see the world differently, even on the same subjects—food, sex, shopping, and, yes, sports.

A dude wouldn't care, and might not even notice, if he and his friend Larry wore the exact same slacks and polo to a company party thrown by the top execs, but two wives wearing the same dress is bound to be an "Oh, crap!" moment.

And that's okay. Really, it is. Take a deep breath, Twitter. It's all true, and nobody needs to think about jumping off a bridge after hearing it.

As a matter of fact, it's understood in comedy writing that people don't laugh if they think they're being taught something. They laugh at societal truths presented to them in humorous ways. Here's the formula: the comedian tells the audience something it already knows to be true, embellishing it along the way, and a hearty laugh follows. Something like—I don't know— women freaking out over wearing the same dress to a company Christmas party.

I pitched a comedy pilot based on my dealings with three strong, opinionated women: my ex-wife, my wife, and a feisty and attractive television cohost at ESPN. During my pitch, the two CBS execs said the women in my show would be too strong. They'd overpower the man, they said. The man—me, to be exact—needed to be stronger, because opinionated women shown dominating weaker or slightly passive men turns off audiences. Oh, wait—I forgot to mention an important point: both of those CBS executives were women.

Their opinions weren't misogynistic; they were simply television reality, based on actual research.

Look, nobody is suggesting that *Men's Health* should be nominated for a National Magazine Award for exposing the dark secret of gender-related sports fandom. But the intent wasn't cruel or mean spirited. It didn't mock anybody or insult an entire gender. Instead, it offered lighthearted suggestions for the millions of men who are married or dating women who lack the same intense stats-driven passion.

These days, though, context is a rarity. Contemplation is an endangered species. Knee-jerk reactions, fake urgency, and sheer volume win the day.

*Men's Health* figured it out too late. Maybe the magazine should have taken the easy route and opted for the masturbation angle.

# INDY FILM

**T**HIS IS THE STORY of a city that goes to bed early and gives every appearance of being a place from a bygone era. Its downtown streets are wide and clean. Its appetites veer more toward traditional steakhouse than vegan fusion. Its sports fans still cheer basketball the way it used to be, appreciating a hard backdoor cut as much as or more than an alley-oop dunk. The fundamentals of everything matter in this town, and a handshake—not a signed contract—is good enough to close a deal.

But there's something else going on in Indianapolis, something that is harder to explain. Its professional athletes get in trouble. And not just "Oh, well, boys will be boys," but real trouble. More trouble, in fact, than the professional athletes in just about any other city in the nation.

Over the last fifteen years, the NBA's Pacers and the NFL's

Colts have had more than forty arrests. That's two teams, with roughly seventy men per year, and roughly three arrests per year.

It's even more shocking when you consider that for many of those years, the Colts were led by the stable and fatherly hand of former head coach Tony Dungy and the stern, no-bullshit approach of former general manager Bill Polian. This is an organization with an eye for details. On the field, same thing: Peyton Manning is the most paternal of NFL quarterbacks. And yet, amid that same locker room, it was a frigging fireworks show of off-field issues.

There were shootings. Someone punched a pizza delivery guy. Drugs, gun charges, DUIs, assaults—these guys had the penal code down pat. Even the owner, Jim Irsay, has been in trouble with the league and the law. And despite Irsay's issues, this isn't a case of an odious owner developing an anything-goes culture throughout the roster of one team.

The Pacers, meanwhile, managed to hold their own. They became such a notorious group that fans did a good job of ignoring them for years as they rose to become a powerhouse in the Eastern Conference. They won games and curtailed their off-court troubles, and yet attendance and local television ratings placed in the bottom third of the league.

I think there's something more insidious at work here. I grew up in a small town, and the common narrative in Podunk, USA, goes like this: big cities are intimidating, dangerous, and filled with potential pitfalls. Parents in the cozier places in our nation have been preaching that gospel since the industrial age, but it fails to take into account a competing yet equally valid narrative: boredom and youth is one of those combinations—like kleptomania and shopping malls—that never seem to end well.

From 2010 to 2015, it wasn't the New York Jets, New Orleans Saints, or Houston Texans getting into trouble. The teams in those cities, filled with countless VIP lounges and late-night clubs and fleshly temptations, were routinely among the bottom three in arrests. At the top? The Minnesota Vikings, Jacksonville Jaguars, and Cincinnati Bengals.

Those aren't bastions of nightlife. Minneapolis, proud of its "Minnesota Nice" reputation, is a city of eternally smiling blond people. Cincinnati is Des Moines with a bigger river. Jacksonville once hosted a Super Bowl and was so ill equipped for the task that cruise ships were called in to serve as hotels.

What happens to pro athletes in places such as Indianapolis is really nothing out of the ordinary. Players are mostly in their early to midtwenties. After intense games and practices, they're looking for places to unwind. Clubs and lounges in the bigger cities can provide that outlet, and do it with a level of civility and security. If the city lacks those places, though, players are going to take the party home, where there's no bouncer, no management concerned with liability, no threat of removal for disrespecting other guests. At the club, the club makes the rules. At home, *you* make the rules. Or, even worse, nobody does.

There were 244 arrests, citations, or charges involving college football players in 2014, according to the Arrest Nation website. Universities such as Iowa State, Oklahoma State, Washington State, Texas A&M, East Carolina, Missouri, Florida State, Maine, and Northern Alabama—all located in smaller, supposedly sleepier cities—were disproportionately represented among those 244 transgressions. Universities in livelier urban centers—UCLA, USC, the University of Nevada–Las Vegas, the University of Miami—were far less likely to be represented in the local police blotter.

There's a corollary at work here that goes against everything your small-town mother preached. If your city has a more vibrant nightlife, helped by a warmer climate coupled with fewer ordinances after nine o'clock, it can lead to fewer off-field disasters and embarrassments. In places where the sidewalks roll up early and watching planes land qualifies as entertainment, keep your eyes open and be ready to dial 911.

Indianapolis is undoubtedly a wonderful place to raise children. I'm sure it's full of hospitable, responsible people who would eagerly lend you their lawn mower in a heartbeat, but it's a far different place for outsiders who land in town after being drafted by a local team or traded to one. They have free time, a stressful job, relentless energy, and money to spend. They're young, and they'll make some regrettable choices, as we all did or will.

How else can you explain the problems experienced by so many Pacers and Colts? A well-run franchise with a stable culture is still no match for young, wealthy players who are usually bored out of their collective minds. It's not a life-defining flaw, though. Eventually they'll learn to like a perfectly cooked steak with a glass of cabernet. They'll appreciate a well-executed give-and-go. They'll understand the value of a meaningful hand-shake. Until then, though, you probably want to root for your friends or family members to be drafted by teams in the glamour cities—maybe New York or Miami—if you want them to stay out of trouble. It doesn't make sense, but that doesn't mean it's not true.

# HORSES AREN'T ATHLETES. THEY'RE BEAUTIFUL, OBSOLETE TRANSPORTATION.

# CHARLES IN CHARGE

**C**HARLES BARKLEY WENT ON a nerd-clubbing expedition during a TNT basketball broadcast one night in February. It was a mistake on many levels—too broad, too harsh—and not the least of which was: they're going to own the entire world at some point, so why rile them up?

But let me take you back to the not-so-subtle salvoes fired indiscriminately by the most reliable funny-talker in sports broadcasting.

"All these guys who run these [NBA] organizations who talk about analytics, they have one thing in common," he said. "They're a bunch of guys who ain't never played the game, and they never got the girls in high school, and they just want to get in the game. The NBA is about talent."

For starters, that's two things, Charles, but we're not here to quibble. Secondly, the word *analytics* might sound all intellectual and scary, but it's really nothing more than patterns of data. You know: information based on performance. I can even simplify it in basketball terms for those who find the word a bit too—how shall I put it?—*math-y*.

Golden State Warriors point guard Stephen Curry, according to analytics, should not be left open. Does that make it any easier?

With that said, though, Barkley's fulminations contained some truth. Talent *is* king in basketball. The sport is just different that way.

In baseball, the best lineup and the strongest starting pitching can be undermined by a lousy bullpen. In football, even the best quarterback—I'm thinking Tom Brady during the early stages of 2014—can't generate first downs if his offensive line struggles. Basketball, on the other hand, is overwhelmingly dominated by the power of one or two.

LeBron James was talented enough to turn a Miami Heat team with an average bench, no center, and a mediocre point guard into a two-time NBA champion. The minute he leaves to return to the Cleveland Cavaliers in 2014, virtually the same roster—complete with a heavy reliance on analytics by coach Erik Spoelstra and the addition of talented forward Luol Deng—can't win with any level of consistency in the wretched Eastern Conference.

Kobe Bryant has won five titles. Analytically speaking, he takes more bad shots in a week than many do in a season. He dribbles too much and dominates the ball on the wing too often for a two-guard, which means his team often comes to a complete standstill when he's doing his thing. But Kobe's talent requires the assistance of precisely zero of his teammates. He rises above the analytics.

You can count the number of superstars who have captured twelve of the last fifteen titles on three fingers: Kobe, LeBron, and Tim Duncan. Astonishingly, fifteen of the last sixteen NBA Finals have featured at least one of those three players. They don't seem to have a ton in common, but they have this: they played on championship teams that had major flaws. Both Duncan and LeBron won titles on rosters that appeared too old and injury plagued. Kobe's former teammate and fellow superstar Shaquille O'Neal was one of the sorriest free-throw shooters in league history, and opponents turned it into a legitimate strategy. Hitting those free throws, as you might expect, is sort of important down the stretch in close playoff games.

The small number of players on a basketball roster makes it statistically impossible to track certain factors. In any business, the smaller the study group—or roster, in our case—the greater the chance for one negative personality to destroy performance.

Think of it as a company Christmas party. You work for an insurance giant with more than thirty thousand employees. You might spend all night at the party, mingling from beginning to end, and never even hear about the fistfight in the bathroom between Bob in sales and Bill in accounting.

But if you're working for a small law firm and one partner

humiliates an apprentice in front of the group, it will not only resonate for the next few weeks but also perhaps create chasms that last years.

In other words, one selfish jerk-off can erode a team in ways you can't measure. And one giving ambassador can have the opposite effect.

In football, offensive players can go long stretches of the season without communicating with defensive players in meetings. Their lockers are in separate parts of the room. At halftime, they often head to different sides of the room—or different rooms altogether. The rules of the game separate players from different sides of the ball.

In baseball, relief pitchers hang out in the bullpen, far from the rest of their teammates in the dugout. There are so many different ethnicities on an average roster that different languages fly constantly around the clubhouse.

In basketball, though, different story. Everyone must share one relatively small locker room and one round leather ball that everybody wants to shoot. The willingness of the star to share and collaborate with the group—and not just in scoring—can either unify or detach a team over the course of a long season.

Basketball's culture has always centered on elevating the superstar. He has unquestioned and almost unlimited influence in the locker room. He's isn't just one of the guys, and nobody criticizes him for acknowledging that. In fact, in a twist that couldn't be fathomed in the other two sports, superstars get hammered by the media when they *aren't* selfish. They *must* take all the crucial shots or else feel the wrath. It's an accepted reality of the sport.

They're watched closer in other areas, too. How hard do they work at practice? Do they pick up the check on the road? Do they create tension with their coaches or dilute it?

Point guard Rajon Rondo of the Sacramento Kings is a unique talent, and one of the league's moodier players. He ignites small fires that don't make the news but manage to become distractions. He is a divider, whereas a player like Magic Johnson was a uniter. Why were teams always magically better when guard Chauncey Billups was around? That's easy: he was one of the more likable and respected players of the past fifteen years. Stars admired him. They listened to him.

NBA stars with attitudes are similar to minor but persistent sleep deprivation. The drawbacks are minimal at first, but over time, work and relationships suffer with the passing of each groggy day. Eventually you're looking at a full-blown crisis.

Right here is where I need to inform you that I believe Carmelo Anthony is one of the most overrated players in the history of the league. Statistics and advanced metrics can't tell the real story. Melo never truly committed to the game. He talked a big game but played another, routinely half-assing it on defense and showing a halfhearted commitment to physical conditioning. You can easily identify the players who put in the work in the weight room before and after practice: Dwyane Wade, Russell Westbrook, Kawhi Leonard, LeBron—stars who put their commitment on display nightly. You can tell just by looking at the shape and definition of their bodies. Just like the rest of us, there's no hiding the truth.

Melo? Not so much. He's always been a little soft during his best moments and downright doughy during his worst. Combine that with a casual approach on defense, and the Knicks star sends a message without saying a single word. Given time with him on the roster, his Knick teams tend to get worse. Players talk and watch. They see a superstar cutting corners, and pretty soon one of two things happens: (1) that ethos spreads or (2) resentment sets in. After Anthony publicly orchestrated a trade from Denver to New York two-thirds of the way through the 2010–11 season, the comments from his ex-teammates and other NBA players spoke volumes about their lack of respect for him. They can be summed up by Milwaukee Bucks forward Chris Dudley, who came on my radio show in late May of 2015 and called Anthony the most overrated player in the league. "He's got to make guys better, and defensively, he's got to take the next level up."

Which brings us back to Billups. The one time that Carmelo had real success is when he shared a plane and a locker room with Billups in Denver from 2008 to 2011. With the two of them in the lineup, the Nuggets won fifty-four and fifty-three games—the two most in Melo's career—and were in the midst of a 50-win season when they were traded in 2010–11. The two were traded to New York together, and Melo had his most successful stretch as a Knick during the final third of that 2010–11 season. How did it work? Billups, the good guy and conflict-resolution specialist, smoothed things out and made it easier for Melo to concentrate on the things he does best. Once Chauncey was waived during the 2011–12 season, coincidence of all coincidences, things deteriorated quickly the following year. There is no numerical pattern that can detect that kind of phenomenon.

Today just look at the Knicks; in 2014–15 they were the second-worst team in the league. Melo's body has fallen apart. He still only pretends to play defense. A couple of his former Knicks teammates, Iman Shumpert and J. R. Smith, have left him and—lo and behold—become better players elsewhere. The perfect example of Melo's philosophy came during the 2015 All-Star Game. He played in the game—it was in New York, after all—and then shut it down for the rest of the season to have surgery and get ready for next year. How do you think that looked from inside the locker room?

An NBA general manager once told me, "It's not about getting a star in this league; it's about getting the *right* star." There are few stars who have ever been more wrong than Carmelo Anthony. Analytics can tell you he takes some questionable jumpers, but little else.

Charles Barkley was partially right during his on-air diatribe that night in February. But guess what? The data collectors are partially right, too. It's about the talent, and some data patterns really do uncover talent with a clarity the eye can't see.

As for who gets the girls? I think it's best if I leave that for someone else to answer.

# AIR TIME

**T**HE DAY LOOKED SUNNY and bright from the inside of the airport, but everything seemed to change when we boarded the flight from Providence, Rhode Island, to Nantucket, Massachusetts, on Cape Air. The wind was howling, strong enough that I swore it bounced the plane a bit as it sat on the tarmac. Every seat was taken, and by "every seat," I mean all eight of them—even the one next to the pilot.

So yeah, it was one of *those* flights, the kind where they weigh the luggage. On this one, they might have even weighed the in-flight magazine along with it. We weren't going to be in the air more than thirty minutes, which is usually good news for my wife, Ann, who's a nervous flyer on the best of days. But on this day, with the wind—and especially the pilot—her anxiety was ramped up.

Now, about the pilot: he wasn't drunk, and he wasn't scruffy. His shoes and belt looked new, and his aviator glasses weren't knockoffs.

The problem? His age. He looked eleven, but in defense of Cape Air, he was probably at least thirteen. The way my wife assessed the situation, she was putting her life in the hands of someone who was only three months removed from hosting a birthday party with a bouncy house. I guess you could say his SpongeBob keychain didn't help calm her fears, either.

The flight turned out fine, and the scarring on my wrist from Ann's death grip is now barely visible. But was her apprehension about the pilot's obvious inexperience unjustified? Think about this: in 2015, you can't rent a car if you're under twenty-five, but you can fly a commercial jetliner with two hundred people onboard on any worldwide carrier if you're in your twenties.

When a twenty-seven-year-old copilot, Andreas Lubitz, murdered 150 passengers and crew on a Germanwings flight in late March 2015 by locking his pilot out of the cockpit and then methodically and deliberately crashing the plane into a French mountainside, one aspect of the tragedy evaded critical assessment: this was a discount airline, where the fares are cheaper and, therefore, so are the people flying the plane. Lubitz had struggled with depression—a condition not reserved for young pilots—but did the cost-cutting airline have the personnel and resources to deal with his mental health issues? We want lower fares, sure, but do we realize they are accompanied by a decision to let less-experienced people control our fate?

In the 2009 Colgan Air crash near Buffalo, where a plane carrying forty-nine people crashed into a house, crew fatigue was cited as a primary cause. Fatigue, of course, often leads to pilot error, which is the leading cause of airline crashes.

Over a two-year span beginning in 2005, Delta Air Lines pilots took two double-digit pay cuts that forced many veteran pilots into retirement. Less-seasoned men and women, who dealt with growing animosity from the airline's most experienced and valued employees, replaced them in the cockpit.

We all read stories about robots replacing up to a quarter of the jobs in the country over the next twenty or thirty years. We've come to assume that self-driving cars are inevitable. It's understood within the airline industry that technological advancements have created planes that require less and less from pilots the second the aircraft lifts off the ground. But that doesn't remove the fact that we want talented people doing these jobs for those rare times when quick-thinking expertise is necessary.

In more than thirty years of flying, I've experienced just a handful of harrowing moments, such as the approach into Memphis when lightning struck the tarmac right before landing, and the pilots shrewdly pulled up the plane—prompting a collective gasp from passengers—and landed us perfectly fifteen minutes later as the ugly electrical storm blazed around us; or the landing in Chicago where an oncoming plane caused our plane to veer so sharply that we could hear the physical stress the torque created on the plane before we safely and elegantly touched down as everyone's sweat was drying.

Pilots are similar to gifted surgeons. They're compensated not just for daily flights but for their skills in crises, which may be needed only once or twice annually.

Many of the smartest young people pursue careers in technology because of the potentially tremendous payoff, which makes me wonder what kind of applicant the airlines will attract if they continue to devalue the job and cut pay. With the proliferation of discount airlines, is there a chance our skies will be filled with second-tier talent? Glorified bus drivers?

A pilot's job doesn't begin with takeoff. It's a series of pre-flight checks and constant training to remain certified. Doesn't that alone indicate the knowledge and expertise necessary for the job?

I always make a point of thanking my pilots as I leave the plane. I want them to know I appreciate their service as well as that dash of gray at the temples and those wrinkles around the eyes. They signify not only age but also experience—the kind we deserve at thirty-three thousand feet, with stormy weather on the horizon.

# EVERY TIME A FAN RUNS ONTO THE FIELD, THE GAP BETWEEN PLAYERS AND FANS GROWS.

# PURR-FECT EXPLANATION

**I**T WAS A PERFECT SATURDAY NIGHT in Las Vegas, which is another way of saying it was a Saturday night in Las Vegas. I was a young, single sportscaster at the time, and I don't remember any other kind.

My girlfriend at the time was named Kitten, although I'm still not entirely sure whether that was her given name or just something she told me. Ancestry.com hadn't come into being yet, and I had no pressing interest in tracking down the truth or history of her family's heritage. So Kitten it was.

I didn't need a birth certificate to know this about her: she ran with a little edgier crowd than I did. I justified this in my twenty-two-year-old brain by figuring I was fit enough and young enough to jump out of a second-story window if the need arose.

On this particular Saturday night in Las Vegas, I remember

the carpet in the front room was gray and the cocaine in the room leading to the coat closet was white. Ever since childhood, I recall colors during moments of crisis, regardless of whether the crisis is mine. The couch I sat on during the O. J. Simpson verdict in 1995 was brown. I was riding in a Cadillac with a light blue interior when CBS Radio reported the explosion of the space shuttle *Challenger* in 1986. The carpet was burnt orange and the blood bright red when I banged my forehead into my father's nose as I sat on his lap when I was five.

And so it came to be that gray and white were the primary colors of this Saturday night. Oh, and one other hypothetical color popped into my head: orange, the color of the prison jumpsuit I'd be wearing if the cops showed up.

I calmly yet forcefully told Kitten that I would rather spend the rest of my life somewhere other than a jail cell, and I darted out of there after forty-five minutes of drinks and appetizers. I probably spent the next several hours hoping someone would hurry up and invent Applebee's, where I would at least feel safe while eating.

There's a message inside the story, and it resonates to this day: not every party is built for every person or group.

I'm hoping this message doesn't get lost when it comes to deciding the college football Final Four in the next decade. The debate will be spirited, no doubt, but we can't let truth be a casualty of the process. Fans—and especially the narrative-defining media—need to remember that certain people shouldn't be invited to certain parties.

If you turn your head just right, you can hear it already: *Give the little guy a chance*. Whatever you do, don't forget what the Boise State Broncos did to big, bad Oklahoma in the 2007 Fiesta Bowl, pulling off a daring 2-point conversion for a thrilling 43–42 victory in overtime. And remember when the University of Utah upset the University of Alabama in the 2009 Sugar Bowl, 31–17?

I remember it, in all its red-and-white glory, and I'm here to tell you why Utah is the perfect example of why teams from second-tier conferences *shouldn't* be invited to that exclusive club. I'll tell you why the occasional upsets don't paint an accurate portrait of much of anything. In fact, the opposite is true: they create a false impression. They mess with your mind.

For the better part of two decades, from 1995 to 2010, Utah was a sturdy pillar of excellence in the Mountain West Conference. The Utes had a fun offense and good coaching and a knack for turning under-the-radar recruits into really good players. Utah finished no worse than third thirteen times in sixteen years. During an eight-year stretch, it never had a losing record, and the team went 21-3 in its final three years in the MWC.

And then what happened?

In 2011 the Utes joined the Pac-12, that's what.

Guess what? Everything changed.

Utah went 7-11 in its first two seasons in conference play, and that's without playing either Stanford or Oregon, the two best teams. It received an exquisitely wrapped scheduling gift and still languished.

If you look beyond wins and losses, you can peel away layers that get closer to the heart of things. Not only has Utah been an also-ran in the Pac-12, it has been an also-ran riddled with injuries. The Utes have struggled to keep their young quarterbacks healthy, and that has more to do with competition than lousy luck.

Fans of Cinderella teams have chronic myopia when it comes to the effect of the constant barrage of violent hits from the physically superior players in major conferences. After the conference expanded to twelve teams, the coach of one of those teams said, "Those teams are a little bigger, stronger, and faster." The coach? Utah's own Kyle Whittingham.

Week in and week out, a team in the Pac-12 or SEC gets pounded. Depth is vital. In a conference such as the Mountain West, you can open and close the season with major power without facing the same kind of weekly physical thrashing. Sure, Utah—the plucky, lovable underdog—was energized against heavily favored Alabama, but what if the Utes had to face Florida seven days later and Auburn seven days after that?

It sounds so simple that it borders on elementary, but it comes down to talent. At the start of the 2013 NFL season, eleven defensive backs had come from Louisiana State University *alone*. Six SEC schools had more than twenty-five players on NFL rosters. A Mountain West team in 2011—Utah's magical, mystical undefeated season—might go successive weeks without facing a single future NFL body.

It's a game of violence, and major conferences simply have

more NFL-level athletes, which translates to more injuries. The road to that Final Four is harsh, mentally and physically; a battle of attrition. Getting to the end means navigating top coaches and elite defenses and road games in front of 94,000 vicious fans cheering on large, angry men.

The average road crowd that Utah faced during the 2011 season was 26,400. That's a tailgate party in Tuscaloosa, a crowd at the bar in Gainesville, a section of the stands in Baton Rouge. Imagine the fury generated by nearly 27,000 fans—could they even make enough noise to disrupt a séance?

We have many opportunities to fight for inclusion in our country, plenty of causes to adopt. Demand it for social services and health care. Take to the streets to improve the living conditions of underprivileged kids.

But please, leave college football's Final Four to the big boys. It isn't a safety net and shouldn't be treated as one. It's a VIP club, where there are rope lines within rope lines, and only the most deserving and tested should have access to the innermost circle.

Do everyone a favor and check your sentimentality at the door. Otherwise there's bound to be a bunch of undeserving teams that'll look back someday and remember only colors.

# SLOW AND STEADY

**H**OW DO WE MAKE SENSE of the feelings we have when our teams win? You feel overwhelming joy when your team finishes off a championship season, and it's quite possible you broke down and cried. Is this some deep-seated coping mechanism to offset our internal insecurities, or could it be the healthiest of outlets for genuine emotion?

People who don't connect with sports don't get it. They see it as silly, or odd, or maybe even beneath them. But that doesn't make it any less real when a Ravens fan in Baltimore feels like he's hovering above the ground for a few hours after his team beat the 49ers in Super Bowl XLVII. And it's not like the fans in San Francisco don't understand: from 2010 through 2014, they levitated three times in five seasons, thanks to the baseball Giants.

What's behind this phenomenon? Does it validate our wisdom of choosing a city, or a franchise, that produces champions? Is their success a reflection of our loyalty to those players, those men we watch nightly until they become like an extended network of cousins? Is that how their joy becomes ours?

It doesn't matter where all of this originates or what part of our psyche controls irrational fandom. What matters is that we've all felt it and hope to feel it again.

Scale doesn't matter. The high school football title means as much to the city of Odessa, Texas, as the NCAA basketball championship does in Durham, North Carolina.

Those two competing feelings—the inexplicable joy of sharing in success and the illogical pain of defeat—define and unite us as sports fans. And so as the college basketball season wound down, and we were inundated with doomsayers decrying the game's slow pace and terrible offenses and hypercontrolling coaches, there was an underlying question that nobody thought to ask:

Is it possible that everybody is trying to fix a problem that doesn't exist?

Too often, we ignore the sociology of college basketball. I've been guilty of it myself. The residents of these smaller towns prefer their basketball to be more team oriented and less flashy. They want to see players who rely more on efficiency than on talent, and they actually relish a system where an older coach controls younger players. That construct, right or wrong, is a better fit for the sensibilities of those communities than the star-driven, clear-a-side isolation game that dominates the NBA. Despite the itinerant nature of the college game, people in Lawrence, Kansas, or Syracuse, New York, feel more connected to the style their program employs, as well as the players enacting it.

Small towns attract people for any number of reasons. Life is slower and presumably simpler. There is a greater sense of community—fewer people means more familiar faces to see at the church or the grocery store. For many people, tradition and comfort trump professional triumph; to them, a good job in Lawrence is worth more than a great job in Saint Louis. Having fewer entertainment options just means more shared life experiences, and probably less anxiety over missing out on unaffordable events or parties that might be deemed "good for the career" somewhere else.

When you watch Wisconsin Badgers fans in Madison, do they seem less connected to their local stars? Less interested in the product? It seems pretty easy to argue that the members of Wisconsin's basketball team, most of them playing in their home state in front of people who have known of them since before they sprouted hair under their pits, have a much stronger connection to the fan base than most pro players do. Put it this way: Is Madison's bond with forward Sam Dekker stronger than Oklahoma City's with high-fashion, high-performance, multimillionaire point guard Russell Westbrook of the Thunder?

We can argue the particulars of the college game until we're drowning in granular details. Sure, scoring is down, and there are way too many time-outs that interrupt the flow. Coaches sometimes go overboard dictating every single possession. But some gentle tweaking of the rules—allow less clutching and grabbing, for one—would go a long way toward healing the current ills. Besides, the nostalgia for higher scores isn't rooted solidly in reality. Wild shootouts have always been the domain of the pro game, as a simple check of Final Four scores over the past two decades shows. There have been far more 74–69 games than 104–102s.

Sure, the game is slower in Charlottesville, Virginia.

So is life.

There's no denying that college basketball was filled with more high-end juniors and seniors years ago, but the college game has always had an appreciation for the well-timed change of pace. Wasn't Villanova University's 1985 title game upset of Georgetown University considered a coaching masterpiece by Rollie Massimino? His team, it should be noted, attempted fewer than thirty shots and made a remarkable 78 percent of them on its way to becoming the lowest-seeded team to win the NCAA Tournament. Pete Carrill created the Princeton offense, a slow-developing, pass-heavy style of play dependent on precise back cuts. Sounds horrible, right? But then why is Carrill considered a visionary, a man fawned over by every sports journalist who's ever spoken into a microphone or earned a byline? And how about the late Dean Smith, who guided the University of North Carolina at Chapel Hill from 1961 through 1997? The most hallowed basketball coach in college history was feted and honored for popularizing the four corners offense—basically glorified keep-away—and now, all these years later, a slowdown tactic or two is a sign of pending doom?

It's a transitional sport. Empowered stars bolt the college game after their mandatory one-year service commitment, but even that angle gets overplayed. The majority of players who leave their programs after one or two years come from the same ten programs. The rosters at Duke, Kentucky, and North Carolina can change like stock prices on a busy trading day, but they deflect focus from an overlooked fact: there are more than 350 Division I basketball programs, and 330 of them will never recruit a player with the talent to leave before his senior year.

Critics point to another number, too: attendance. It's down on college campuses, but that's not solely a hoops issue. Football programs have been noticing the downward trend for years, even at top-twenty programs where students can watch games on giant flat-screen televisions in their dorms or frat houses while monitoring social media. Being at the game might be a one-of-a-kind experience, but there's something to be said for pausing the game while you walk to the fridge for a beer. How about this zany solution to the attendance issue: scale down the size of stadiums and arenas. Does a rural town with a population of 23,000 really need a 98,600-seat monstrosity looming over campus?

The 2015 version of March Madness set cable television ratings records, some of them attributed to the University of Kentucky's failed attempt at an undefeated season. Still, it's almost always true that television ratings in any sport rise and fall based on the significance of the teams involved. College hoop fans could just as easily refer to the troubles the NBA had in its post–Michael Jordan world, where the league was as appealing as a woolen sweater sale in Phoenix.

Could it be possible that the national media, along with the major metropolitan markets, are disconnected from the interests and inspirations of people in less hectic places such as College Station, Stillwater, or Lexington? Is there room for places where the strong-willed, no-nonsense, regimented coach is exactly what appeals to the citizens and fans? Is it within the realm of reason that some players—realizing this is their last chance to play the game in a place where they are loved and respected—actually want to play for one of those domineering winners? Inside that bubble, where they don't care about columnists in New York or talk-show hosts in Los Angeles, they understand how much the college game means to everyone involved.

During his team's run to the championship game, Wisconsin coach Bo Ryan listened to the litany of complaints about today's college basketball game and responded by saying, "I like to switch it around and see all the good things about our game." The problem, as Ryan sees it, isn't with the game; it's with all those who expect it to be something it was never intended to be.

# LET'S BE HONEST:
## CLEVELAND
### DOESN'T REALLY ROCK.

# RETURN TO LENDER

**I'LL ADMIT IT:** I fell for it, just like almost everyone else. Charles Barkley told me later that he'd gotten all choked up as he sat in a hotel room and watched me react to the news. It was LeBron James, in July 2014, informing America he was coming home. Back to depressing and beaten Cleveland, back to save the franchise and the city and the economy and whatever else happened to get in his way. The announcement, written with *Sports Illustrated*'s Lee Jenkins, grabbed your heartstrings and didn't let go.

> *. . . I have two boys and my wife, Savannah, is pregnant with a girl. I started thinking about what it would be like to raise my family in my hometown. I looked at other teams, but I wasn't going to leave Miami for anywhere except Cleveland.*

*The more time passed, the more it felt right. This is what
makes me happy.*

*. . . I want kids in Northeast Ohio, like the hundreds of
Akron third-graders I sponsor through my foundation, to
realize that there's no better place to grow up. Maybe some of
them will come home after college and start a family or open a
business. That would make me smile. Our community, which
has struggled so much, needs all the talent it can get.*

Come on. That's not even fair. It's like a puppy telling its
owner it's sorry for having run away as it leaps back into his
arms. On the air that day, I could barely get through LeBron's *SI*
piece. I paused not for dramatic effect but simply because if I
didn't, I was sure the tears would flow.

Here's the thing, though: You know about Newton's Third
Law? For every action, there is an equal and opposite reaction?
Well, the day LeBron James returned to Cleveland was a really,
really bad day for the NBA. At that very moment, as the announcement was posted online and the world took note, the
league lost its villain. LeBron took off the black hat, placed it on
the ground somewhere in South Beach, and walked toward the
light. He was no longer the guy you claim to hate but can't stop
watching. Oh, during his four seasons as a member of the Heat,
you rooted against him and hated every bit of Miami's glitz and
ego and superficiality and . . . and . . . your hatred—your sput-
tering, irrational hatred—provided emotional satisfaction.

You stopped watching that television show once Simon

Cowell left. You lost a little of your mojo when Major League Baseball forced Alex Rodriguez to sit out a season. You and your spouse gained weight after you got married. They're all connected, in a weird way, to agitation and uncertainty, two really uncomfortable but powerful emotions that LeBron ended—in an NBA sense—when he announced his homecoming.

We're all happy now, and that's what we want to be, but happiness is not what drives us—or our sports—to the highest levels. Villains do. Enemies do. Rivals do. Angst does. You know what drives us? The Yankees' ridiculously exorbitant payrolls of the 1990s and early 2000s did. The ostentatious, rule-flouting Miami Hurricanes of the 1980s—college football's first televised strip club—did. Chest beating and unapologetic dominance not only infuriates us but also intimidates us. And it's great for sports.

Think about your favorite sports moments. Wasn't an enormous part of your elation with the win the fact that someone you deeply despised lost? Part of that feeling was based on the fear that the bad guys might pull away and leave you behind, a second-rate contender. It's Newton's Third Law as applied to sports.

LeBron's move to Miami in 2010 was excessive and self-celebratory, and yet so damned good. The fans and the media pulled hard against him, and, in the process, every winning streak or four-game slide became an event. This is a place where sports and life intersect; what makes us happy often makes us soft and content, and what drives us mad often inspires.

The 2014–15 NBA season, LeBron's first back in Cleveland, had some remarkable moments. Klay Thompson of the Golden State Warriors scored 37 points *in a freaking quarter.* But overall, there was no pizzazz; nobody to root against with a passion that could be mistaken for mental instability. The whole thing's gotten a little too clubby to engender any legitimate hatred. Players work out together in the offseason, so the hatred that was so real—and so prominently displayed when Michael Jordan was trying frantically to topple the Bad Boy Detroit Pistons in the late 1980s—is long gone.

The 2014–15 season had emerging teams like the Washington Wizards, Toronto Raptors, and Atlanta Hawks semidelivering on their long-simmering potential. Golden State could be a blast to watch, and the Bulls now have several players who can actually put the ball in the basket, even though Derrick Rose continues to show an inability to keep his cartilage and ligaments in proper order.

But did any of those storylines and subplots send you rushing to a television? Well, apparently not, since ratings for both TNT and ESPN were down.

LeBron bolted back to Cleveland and wrote an emotional essay that had us all thinking about the inherent goodness of man. Cleveland restaurants probably sell more steaks on game night, and the city has some of its buzz back. Even Cavaliers owner Dan Gilbert, he of the comic sans diatribe against his departing star four years earlier, apologized for having let his angry side show. Good for them—good for all of us—but bad for the league. You can feel the loss of energy. Someone unplugged the hate, and we all lost power.

Maverick Carter, a longtime friend of LBJ's and now a prominent member of his management team, sat in my office one afternoon. I poked and prodded him for an hour on his friend's move back to northeast Ohio. *It just felt right* was the general, almost grudging, consensus. It's hard to tell what the country's most renowned athlete is thinking before a big decision. ESPN's Stephen A. Smith told me that LeBron didn't make up his mind to bolt Cleveland for Miami until the morning he did it.

LeBron sat down in Miami Beach with Gilbert, a billionaire who'd said horrible things to help light a national fire on James's property, and he forgave him. I can't hold that against anyone; moving on is a very healthy thing.

The whole operation was just so tidy. It was as close to a fairy tale as sports is likely to give us. All was forgiven. All the rough edges were sanded down. That's why I fell for it. That's why I got caught up in the kind of sentimental moment that I so often preach for fans to avoid. Lee Jenkins and LeBron got me, and they got Charles Barkley, and they got almost everyone in the predominantly cynical sports media. We're all happier now, right? All is right with the world. Boredom won. The happy ending gets a parade.

Yep, I nearly cried. Crying is good for adult men, or so they tell me. It releases enzymes or protons or something, but I miss the Miami scene and the swagger and the tense feeling that the entire country was waiting for the Heat to stumble. If they lost, you pumped your fist and won that day's argument.

But in the end, we both won. Maybe that says something about me. Or maybe it says something about you. Or maybe we're all in this together.

# AARON SOME GRIEVANCES

**O**BSTINATE AND OUTRAGEOUSLY TALENTED, Randy Moss didn't seem like a natural fit with the stoic and covert New England Patriots. Then again, neither did the attention-seeking Chad Ochocinco (née Johnson). Moss left a much greater imprint on the team, even though neither of them lasted long. The Patriots jettisoned both as soon as they hit their expiration date, and what happened to these two famous wide receivers afterward was telling.

Absolutely nothing. That's what happened.

Throughout their respective careers, both Moss and Ochocinco were loud and dissenting voices with little regard for repercussions or punishment, and yet neither of them could muster even a mildly snippy sound bite about Tom Brady after they were sent packing. In fact, the Patriots have washed their hands of several of Brady's targets over the years—some of them with good years left in them—and all leave with nothing but pleasant memories and kind words for their quarterback.

The same goes for Peyton Manning. Sure, he can be controlling and tough on less-motivated teammates, and yet every tight end and wideout who has played with him speaks of the experience in hushed, reverential tones. Dozens of players have had their chance to sling an arrow or two, and none has.

No unpleasant mudslinging in the direction of the New Orleans Saints' Drew Brees or San Diego Chargers quarterback Philip Rivers, either.

But up in Green Bay, Wisconsin, where an anti-Packers opinion could lead to unrivaled mayhem, all sorts of Aaron Rodgers's former teammates fire away at the Packers' beloved leader. Greg Jennings, a bright and respected receiver, said Rodgers was not team-oriented and had a tendency to put himself above the team. It wasn't the nastiest of nasty quotes, but Donald Driver, another former Rodgers target, followed it by saying that Rodgers was reluctant to take blame. Another unsatisfied customer? Tight end Jermichael Finley, whose agent publicly complained *about* Rodgers. Agents don't do that unless they're told.

Three primary targets, all calling out the best quarterback in the league. Go back and look for yourself; you'll see. It's hard to find even one publicly calling out a top signal caller. Sure, Terrell Owens did, insulting Donovan McNabb when the two were teammates in 2005, but his opinion doesn't count, because he managed to criticize every single man who has ever thrown him so much as a hitch route in a junior varsity scrimmage. Even the enigmatic and heavy-lidded Jay Cutler of the Chicago Bears, a man who has redefined *sour* with his in-game demeanor, a man who has played with mercurial teammates such as Brandon Marshall, has never been tagged publicly.

And yet Rodgers is a serial victim, a regular dartboard for verbal abuse.

These criticisms don't have much impact in the local coverage around Green Bay and Milwaukee. The folks there need to have access to Rodgers and the Packers, after all, and if you burn him once, you're left without a relationship—even a superficial one—with the one guy you need. That's sort of an industry secret, and it dictates what happens when a national reporter or broadcaster breaks an important local story or publicly criticizes a team. The local press stands tall in a show of solidarity. How *dare* those disconnected out-of-towners! They don't have the relationships we have.

Which is exactly the point.

We don't have—or need to have—a relationship with the local big shot. We don't rely on the local car dealer or independent grocer to purchase the ads that pay our bills. We don't need access to any one locker-room hero or disgruntled shooting guard, which means our opinions aren't filtered in a manner that allows them to protect and serve. My greatest allies as a journalist are distance and options.

You don't air your dirty laundry in professional sports; that's the understanding—even when you leave teams. The club is exclusive and private, and what happens behind closed doors is no-body's damned business. The omertà of the clubhouse is why so many Yankees were pissed off about Joe Torre's 2009 book about his managerial days with the team. From the outside, it might have read like it was full of compliments and keen yet benign in-sight. From the inside, Torre's few tactful criticisms made people in the organization furious.

Which brings us back to Rodgers, the most gifted quarter-back in the league. He has an arm Zeus would admire. He can squeeze passes into places a staple gun couldn't. He's immensely popular among fans and nearly iconic on the national stage, and yet three teammates or former teammates had no problem lob-bing grenades in his direction.

And let's be clear: the criticism doesn't originate from rogue sources and off-the-record discussions. It comes from well-known teammates, in the press, all speaking on the record. You don't carve up the Super Bowl stallion—at least not for the whole world to see—unless things were fairly strained.

Why doesn't this get regular play in our twenty-four-hour news-and-analysis cycle? Why isn't it a bigger story? Why have these significant barbs just evaporated?

Packers head coach Mike McCarthy, a widely respected of-fensive mind who works with Rodgers on game plans, told a top football agent that the only difference between Rodgers and Cutler is this: "Rodgers has talent." Two former Packers told me Rodgers is moody, overly sensitive, and doesn't always feel the need to bring his "A" material.

There have been very few criticisms of Rodgers's performance on the field, and only one that seems to be repeated often enough to qualify as a trend: he holds the ball too long. It's hardly a unique or particularly damaging characteristic—in fact, sometimes it's a plus—but it's the *reason* that intrigued me.

One of Rodgers's former teammates told me, "He doesn't want lots of interceptions on his résumé. He's very aware of that. Andrew Luck doesn't give a shit. Luck is totally selfless. It's all about winning at any cost. He could throw six picks, but if the Colts win, he's the happiest guy in the world."

Translation: Aaron could win and throw six picks, but those six picks would bother him because they would make Aaron look bad. The person who issued that analysis wasn't an outsider or a commentator or a guy emailing a radio show. He was a teammate, someone who was in the same offensive huddle many times.

Rodgers has spent six years as a starter, with above-average offensive weapons around him, in a league that rewards offense. What does he have to show for it? For one, he's had consecutive playoff wins in only one season. That alone doesn't make him overrated, but shouldn't it be better? Don't we look at Peyton Manning's playoff record and wonder if there's something missing?

In every sport, there are megatalents who simply lack leadership skills. The three most gifted baseball players of my adult life—Alex Rodriguez, Barry Bonds, and Ken Griffey Jr.—were not considered leaders. Teammates didn't rally around them or seek their counsel in times of crisis. In the NBA, every team has at least one immensely talented player, but how many stars would you consider to be tremendous leaders? Outside of LeBron James, find me one player—just one—who is willing to be disliked by teammates for the sake of team growth and wins.

But Rodgers is a quarterback, and an elite one, and it's not only a shortcoming but also an indictment to be anything less than JFK or Winston Churchill in the leadership department. On Wall Street, in a hospital, in a top law firm, or in any other sport, simply possessing phenomenal talent is enough to make you rich and respected. In some of those professions, being independent and aloof can carry a certain gravitas; a mysterious air that can only elevate the profile: a maverick with a mystique. In the NFL, though, for that one position, you are viewed either as a leader with talent or you don't qualify for all-time greatness.

An NFL quarterback who knows Rodgers and defends him says, "He's too California cool for some players. When you have his talent, you don't need to do it like everyone else." There it is again: he's just doing his own thing. The truth is, Rodgers is an envied talent but a second-tier leader. Is that unfair?

My assessment of Rodgers comes across as criticism even though all I'm doing is printing things actually said about him and making the obvious connections. The process feels similar to what Rush Limbaugh said to his critics who condemned him for being spectacularly one-sided with his opinions. Limbaugh, notorious for deriding what he considers the "left-wing media," responded by saying, "I am the balance."

This chapter isn't a mean-spirited attempt to dig up dirt on Rodgers, but it is an acknowledgment that he is one reason—maybe the biggest reason—the Packers have had just two extended playoff runs in his seven seasons since taking over from Brett Favre in 2008. The insurance commercials are clever, sure, and the arm is rifle-tastic, but he's also the only top NFL quarterback in recent memory to be routinely sandblasted by teammates.

Uniquely gifted, aloof, overly concerned with his stats, a nice guy off the field, unwilling to bail out his teammates—and, once again, watching someone else in the Super Bowl.

Call it what you will, but I'll cut through the fog and call it what it is: Aaron Rodgers. And those aren't criticisms. They're descriptions.

# WE HAVE BECOME

OBSESSED WITH WEAPONS.

# THAT, OR MAYBE

I JUST DON'T REMEMBER

# THE POLICE TANK

IN THE FOURTH OF JULY

# PARADE WHEN I WAS A KID.

# PLAYING THE PERCENTAGES

**I**T WAS ONE ARREST AFTER ANOTHER, with higher-
and higher-profile jocks being led away in handcuffs at an alarming rate, when my wife, Ann, turned to me in bed one morning
as we watched *SportsCenter* and sipped coffee. With a disgusted
look on her face, she asked, "How can you watch all these games
when all the athletes are such creeps?"

It's not an uncommon thought, and after thinking it over for
a second, I decided to go all analytical on her. I tried to explain
that, much like crime in general, we hear more about crime
among athletes because our ever-expanding media universe creates greater transparency. The creep rate hasn't grown, I told her,
as much as the coverage has. In fact, among the demographic
most likely to commit crime—men eighteen to twenty-five—

professional athletes commit significantly fewer violent crimes than others in the age group do.

After more than twenty-five years of watching athletes up close and personal, I have witnessed several trends, and one of the most prominent is the drastic increase in personal wealth and the problems it causes.

Anyone who comes into major jack for the first time feels two competing forces: (1) the suspicion that your exploding income makes you a target, and (2) an unmistakable belief in your own invincibility. Both of those feelings increase exponentially the younger you are. But get ready for a bombshell, because there's one overriding thing I've witnessed about the vast majority of these young athletes: they're really solid people.

They're goal-oriented and focused. Almost all of them come from middle-class or lower economic backgrounds and are driven to attain a better life through sports.

Sure, they can be selfish with their time, but most have careers that last less than a decade. And yes, their egos can be boundless, but some of that is understandable in light of how the starstruck public reacts to their very existence.

The really good guys, like former NBA player Shane Battier and Seattle Seahawks quarterback Russell Wilson, are much more likely to elevate the less fortunate or promote an impressive number of worthy causes. On the other end, athletes who rise up from more chaotic backgrounds often crash just as suddenly. They're the ones left hoping that an uncreative Hollywood producer casts them in a second-rate reality show to temporarily ease the financial free fall.

But the good and decent people far outnumber those who embody whatever the opposite of good and decent might be. In fact, my biggest headaches have usually been initiated by cranky coaches—guys who should know better—and not twenty-four-year-old running backs.

There are sociological patterns at work in sports—even within each individual sport. Over more than two decades in this business, I've observed how the path to the pros in each sport tends to create its own discrete set of behaviors.

Hockey players, often from Canada or the more liberal European countries, tend to drink the most and—in my experience, nothing more—pursue the opposite sex with an unrivaled ferocity. They also have a greater sense of personal fashion and a more expansive, broad-based understanding of the world around them.

NBA players smoke the most pot, although my opinion could be tainted by the years I spent covering the twelve-man cloud that was the Portland Trail Blazers in the late 1990s. NBA players also tend to be the most laid-back and brand conscious. Remember, golf and hoops are the sports where players can make the most money from the equipment they wear, and that creates a universal understanding of the importance of logos. It also, in a related development, creates a delusional sense of personal value.

You know who goes against type? Football players. They're the most mature and well rounded at an early age. The reasons for this are rooted in the sport, of course. NFL players spend at least three years in college; they understand that their careers will be shorter because of the violence in the sport; they tend to start families earlier and develop a bottom-line mentality right away. Football players don't have guaranteed contracts like baseball and basketball players do, so they have an intimate understanding of their sport's ruthless business practices. Underachievement leads directly to unemployment.

Baseball players are, without a doubt, the most insulated. A good number of them go straight from travel baseball to an unglamorous—and nearly completely ignored—minor league experience. It's a closed shop, a tight-knit community that has little or no tolerance for those who haven't paid the same dues. As baseball has become less popular in metropolitan areas in the United States, more players come from rural or suburban backgrounds, and like voters in those types of communities, baseball players veer toward a more traditional approach to life. They cling to the good old days—they *love* the good old days—and they see their sport as the last monolith in the sports world.

Most athletes don't have time to be idiots. Every sport demands virtually year-round training, which eliminates large chunks of down time, which is a very good thing for a twenty-something with megacash and unlimited ways of spending it. I know, this would be a better story if I unveiled the half dozen times I experienced or witnessed rude or disgusting behavior from jocks. And yes, Barry Bonds really was a pill the two times I was assigned to cover him. Is that better? If it is, stop reading now, because I will also that say Bonds's bad behavior wouldn't have risen above the level of rudeness you see from the average airline customer arguing with a gate agent over a delayed flight.

Oh sure, infidelity is rampant and entitlement is everywhere, but these aren't elected officials or people we're trusting to manage our pension funds. They are kids—really, *really* rich kids—who are going through life with cameras and phones documenting their every indiscretion.

There's nothing new happening out there, just new ways of bringing it to your attention. Philadelphia Eagles receiver Riley Cooper shouted a racial epithet at a concert—you think that didn't happen in some form or fashion thirty years ago? Johnny Manziel's bathroom antics in Las Vegas over the Fourth of July weekend in 2014, in which he was photographed rolling up a twenty-dollar bill for the purpose of who-knows-what, is the kind of thing that has taken place since the beginning of time. The difference, as I tried to explain to my wife in my best professorial tone, was the notable lack of iPhones back in the good old days.

Rutgers University basketball coach Mike Rice was fired for kicking and throwing basketballs at his players. You think the Scarlet Knights of 2013 were the first college ballers ever to be beaned by an orange Spalding?

Don't blame the athlete. We're just standing closer, literally and figuratively. We see every pimple and hear every last one of Tom Brady's regular stream of F-bombs.

You wanted access, pal, and now you've got it. Maybe we've misplaced our blame. Instead of coming down hard on the immature tight end, we should point the finger at the late Steve Jobs and the rest of the brilliant engineers at Apple.

# A BRAND-NEW WORLD

**T**HE SCENE WAS JUST ONE MORE company Christmas party for a rock-and-roll radio station—there have been so many through the years that I can't remember which one. And the person in question was one of the more popular disc jockeys—there have been so many through the years I can't remember whether it was one of the Party Martys or a Jerry the Junkyard Dog. This guy distinguished himself only by the arm candy he brought as a date.

After some mingling at the open bar in the nondescript hotel ballroom, everybody gravitated toward the tables and took a seat. This is when things got weird. The disc jockey's girlfriend decided to grab a microphone. She began to sing.

I'm not entirely sure of the sequence of events that led to this moment, but I'm reasonably confident she was allowed to sing because the DJ was really popular. It clearly had nothing to do with her vocal range, because the three minutes that followed her decision to grab the microphone were the most uncomfortable of my life. At one point, she made the transition from singing to screaming. Have you ever heard a wild animal caught in a leg trap? And if so, have you ever wondered what that animal would sound like if it got caught in the trap after several gin-and-tonics?

There were many issues at work here: the absence of self-awareness, the presence of privilege, the possibility of hearing loss. More than anything, though, it was an issue of timing. Had she bombed at the very end of the night, as people were filing out with several cocktails inside them, her performance would have been a bizarre but memorable ending to a great night. You and your date would have howled about it the whole way home. By going off the rails right from the start, she set the tone for the evening. Instead of celebrating the holiday, you were left to whisper, "Whose idea was that?" to everyone you knew.

Timing might not be everything—it also never hurts to be able to carry a tune—but it's very important.

As these things tend to do, the memory of that Christmas party leads me somewhere else: to college football, where prominent quarterbacks are going out of their way to build a brand off the field long before they build anything on it.

They want to cash in, I get it, but their timing's off. After they finish college, and before the draft, they get together with their teams of agents and seek to capitalize on their college success and protect their future earning potential. There's a lot of opportunity out there, from clothing lines to eyewear deals to any number of other branded items that appeal to the fans of these potential stars.

The agents and quarterbacks are so intent on trademarking variations of their names (Johnny Manziel and Jameis Winston) and so busy creating sock lines (Robert Griffin III) and so concerned with photo shoots on the beach with near-naked models (Mark Sanchez) that they create resentment before they pad up for their first professional practice. The most important player in the locker room loses some of his teammates before the first snap.

Football is not an egalitarian sport. The quarterback is not only the highest-paid player but also the one who gets the majority of the endorsement opportunities. Baseball, basketball, and hockey don't work that way: being a small forward doesn't limit your marketing opportunities to start a cologne line, and a left fielder who leads the league in homers is no less appealing to a car company than a first baseman who does the same.

But in football, a guy can block brilliantly for Aaron Rodgers for a decade and never sniff so much as a cat food commercial. New England Patriots offensive tackle Nate Solder can protect Tom Brady's backside through five more Super Bowl wins and still not be recognized outside of a family reunion.

You ever heard of an offensive guard buying his quarterback a Rolex? Nope, because quarterbacks need to take care of the guys who support, and often save, them. Watches, vacation packages, pickups—quarterbacks give and give and never expect anything in return but loyalty and an ability to see the backside blitz. In a way, it's similar to parenting. There are no expectations of reciprocity, just the nagging doubt that you're not being generous enough with your friendship or patience.

Players understand how it works. They know that a quarterback who has some on-field success will be granted public adulation, but chasing it before you earn it raises eyebrows.

Andrew Luck, despite being the number-one pick in the 2012 draft and possessing a last name that's an advertiser's dream, refused early endorsement offers. That type of maturity and self-awareness—not to mention his obvious talent—earned him high marks with teammates. Similarly, Russell Wilson avoided the gilded trappings of the position until after he won not only playoff games but also a Super Bowl. In both cases, mature young men chose to build trust and respect in the locker room before building their grandchildren's bank accounts with endorsement deals. Luck's case is particularly unique: he was so highly prized from the outset that seizing a deal here and there would have been met with a shrugging acceptance.

There are a growing number of examples of quarterbacks doing the exact opposite. From the first month of his pro career with the Washington Redskins, Griffin was the subject of backstabbing and sniping. His Rookie of the Year season was dotted with stories of his ego. Manziel told reporters, "I will never change," when he was asked about his party-boy past. He trademarked several variations of his name. Again, just like RGIII,

Manziel dealt with animosity early and often from Cleveland teammates, some of whom leaked stories about his weak focus on preparation.

Why do these stories get out? Simple: teammates want them to get out. It would be easy for Cincinnati Bengals players to unload their frustrations on QB Andy Dalton, who was handed a loaded roster as a rookie but has proven unable to elevate the players around him. Dalton has been an unmitigated disaster in three playoff starts, but you'd have to search far and wide to find a hint of criticism—even anonymous—from teammates or management.

What protects Dalton and his mediocre talent? His low-key, respectful manner.

Most fans don't understand the interior workings of an NFL team. Short careers and constant violence create a caste system. Even those at the top must pay their respects to those who came before them, and those who currently block for them. Collaboration is key: every player needs every other player. Baseball and basketball are often a series of one-on-one encounters, but football is choreography. Ten players in football can work in concert but be undermined by a guard who moves one inch one millisecond before the snap. Lomas Brown, an elite left tackle from 1985 through 2002, admitted on ESPN that his lack of respect for Lions quarterback Scott Mitchell led him to let a defensive lineman get past him and clobber his teammate. That's some serious business right there.

The rules of being a young, high-profile quarterback are

pretty simple: respect your fellow man and the pain he endures, knowing that you will have time to make your fortune. That time will arrive after you have proven your ability to play at the highest level. It will come when you prove you are a giver first and a taker second. Understand that football players define themselves differently than other people—even other athletes— do. Play hurt or lose respect; show respect or get hurt.

In short, the sock line is secondary to your offensive line. And if they ask you to sing, do everyone a favor and don't. But if you must, wait until the party's winding down.

# "BREAKFAST
## SERVED ALL DAY"
# NEEDS TO BE
## A FEDERAL MANDATE.

# OPPORTUNITY ROCKS

**I**F YOU WOULD KINDLY INDULGE ME, I'd like to take just a few minutes of your time—no more than three or four, tops—to address a very small portion of America.

Forgive me if I seem presumptuous, but consider this a public service announcement. After more than a decade on syndicated radio, a span that includes more than 32,000 minutes talking, 6,500 minutes interviewing, and roughly 146,000 minutes reading emails, I'm still enjoying nearly every minute of it.

Note what I did there: *nearly*.

And this is where the quick PSA makes its appearance. There's a small, almost granular, portion of my listening and viewing audience that I would like to address directly. These outliers appear rarely but predictably, like cicadas, showing up every time society or sports offers a little mayhem. It could be young people protesting authority or an athlete expressing himself loudly and demonstrably.

That's when the calls and emails come flooding in, all carrying the same message:

*This country is dying.*

They talk about moral decay and rising crime rates and the lunacy of a world that's spinning wildly out of control. They usually have names like Stan or Hal—providing helpful generational hints—but not always. They almost always consider themselves the last placeholders of traditional American values.

The violence or unrest they see in Ferguson, Missouri, or the peaceful protests in New York City following a grand jury's decision not to charge the police officer who put Eric Garner in the fatal fifteen-second choke hold is, to them, unprecedented. To a man—and they're almost always men—they've never seen such a thing. This, of course, would come as shocking news to historians who chronicled the violent Old West, lynchings of blacks in the early twentieth century, or the 1970 Kent State University massacre, in which four unarmed student protesters were killed by members of the Ohio National Guard.

I understand that insulting the audience, even the tiniest sliver of it, is bad business. But you know what? I'm rolling the dice anyway, with a little message of my own:

The world isn't dying, partner—you are.

What the world—and this country—is doing is shedding. They've always done this, but this time technology is making it happen at a faster pace. Time and location mean less now, so a police officer shooting an unarmed eighteen-year-old and leaving his body on a street outside St. Louis can ignite nearly immediate protests from New York to Oakland. Business moves at warp speed, and so does social activism. The process is peeling off the rigid and the stubborn, those slow to adjust and unwilling to adapt, and it's going about the task with remarkable swiftness.

The good old days were simpler. Yep, you got me there. You had so few choices that day-to-day decisions were practically made for you. I can't argue with that, either. But let me give you a few examples of this new world that aren't half bad. In fact, let me take you to the Atlanta airport, where a potentially dreadful late-afternoon flight delay provided a four-hour glimpse into the heart of a "dying" country.

Don't get me wrong: the delay wasn't as exciting as a Colorado rafting trip, but let me take you through it. After being informed of the delay, I hopped on my laptop and read a fascinating article in *Wired* magazine, an edgy and smart monthly, on the making of the movie *Argo*. Since airport food options have improved exponentially, I followed my reading with a trip to a restaurant, where I devoured one the best barbecue sandwiches I've had in my adult life. Cost: $6. From there I returned to my gate and watched a Steve Carell movie (free) on technology that didn't exist back when our country was going strong.

My iPhone provided me with constant updates on the status of my flight, allowing me to chill rather than having to ask repeatedly for new information. When my flight finally boarded, I resisted the urge to watch ESPN on the seat-back television and instead put on my noise-reduction headphones and slept like a baby who'd just crawled a 10k.

A car service, one forced to reduce its rates because of competition from services like Uber, got me home within twenty-five minutes of landing. Once I was home, my wife surprised me with a lasagna dinner she ordered from a new, quick, and reasonably priced pasta delivery service.

And that was nothing compared with the next day, when I watched the NFL Red Zone, which gave me every scoring opportunity in the league on one convenient channel. I was planning to drive to work to spend an hour getting ahead for the week, but fortunately my iPhone allowed me to read and edit scripts in just minutes from a really comfortable chair my wife had purchased at Ikea, a discount furniture store that began in Sweden but—thanks to our global economy—has a store within my area code.

Not that I would feel threatened if I had to visit my local furniture retailer, since crime rates have dropped over the last decade in nearly every major city because of improved law enforcement capabilities.

Before bed that night, I opened Twitter, which is free (how cool is that?), and read two articles about my favorite team, the New England Patriots, from writers I had favorited. For the uninitiated, that means I can often read their work before they've even the left the stadium.

My wife was tired from an earlier hike she'd taken with the kids around a local reservoir. Her arthritic wrist was giving her trouble, but a new medication eased the pain quickly. It was the same searing discomfort her grandmother felt daily, without relief, over the last twenty-five years of her life.

So where was I? Oh, yeah: life in 2015 doesn't always suck.

At different points over the past sixty years, everything from rock-and-roll music to pot was destined to take down the nation. Civil unrest and determined protests are signs of a strong, albeit flawed, democracy, not a weakening one.

This wide disconnect, perhaps, is created by 24/7 media outlets, which all too often capitalize on fear. The bored, agitated, and less mobile can sit and watch every terrible crime and every moment of unrest unfold while they work themselves into an unhealthy lather.

They've got it all wrong. The country isn't dying. Some of its people are, though—along with their attitudes.

# ONE MAN'S RISK, ANOTHER MAN'S MIRACLE

**I** **WAS STARING INTO** one of those cheap metal mirrors that state parks use in their bathrooms to avoid the inevitability of broken glass from vandalism. It doesn't give you the clearest reflection, but on that day and in that moment—during a summer afternoon in the early 1980s—that cloudy metal mirror returned an image that a teenage kid with chronic acne never, ever thinks he'll see:

A pimple-free face.

It was magic. Within days of using a drug called Accutane, my ugly blotches and painful bumps had cleared. As I worked my summer job cleaning toilets in the Washington State Park System, those metal mirrors were constant reminders of Accutane's potency. It was my wonder drug, as in "I wonder what it will be like to actually get a girlfriend."

Like anything good, Accutane arrived with caveats. It was a severe drug that came with several warnings and some significant side effects: extreme chapped lips, daunting headaches, potentially suicide-inducing depression. My dermatologist warned me of its dangers, but for a young kid struggling with confidence, I would have resorted to larceny to obtain those shiny pills.

More than three decades later, driving east on I-84 in Connecticut, minding my own business, a public service announcement came on my radio. A serious man with a serious message invited any listener who had used Accutane to join a class-action lawsuit. Tens of millions of dollars were at stake, and yet I had no interest in joining. The benefits that drug provided me, from confidence with girls to a fuller social life, were worth every day it might take from my life in some nebulous future.

Even as a mostly oblivious and distracted seventeen-year-old, I could tell this drug (generic name: isotretinoin) wasn't a heaping bowl of fresh vegetables. It hit like Tyson with loaded gloves. But none of that mattered, because the damned stuff *worked*. I would take that pill, every single morning, all over again.

And that's the precise sentiment former NFL Pro Bowl offensive tackle Tony Boselli—and dozens of other former players—conveyed to me when I asked why he never joined the class-action lawsuit against the NFL that alleged the league hid the damages of brain injury caused by the game. "I knew the risk and would lie to get on the field," Boselli told me. "I just loved the game." Boselli was one of the best offensive linemen to play the game; he was also one of the smartest.

He's not alone, either. "I never once thought strapping on a fiberglass helmet and running at full speed into large men was great for me," Hall of Famer Howie Long said. "But everything I have I owe to football."

Consumption for pleasure is a complicated issue. What someone is willing to ingest or risk physically for the rush of an immediate payoff varies from person to person. Amid that ever-changing equation, a question arises: If you decide to take the drug or play the game, how much of the responsibility for the consequences falls on you?

Does anyone really think an energy drink, a can of soda, or a piece of cake is good for your health? Sugar, according to a recent study on heart disease, has a direct correlation with early death. The marketers of candy bars certainly never gave me a heads-up on that one. Every Coke and Pepsi ad makes it look like anyone who consumes those products lives a joyous and risk-free existence. I won't even mention fast-food joints. Ever since I watched the 2004 documentary *Super Size Me*, I go into convulsions every time I drive past one.

And let's agree to avoid the topic of alcohol consumption altogether. It's rife with health risks, but it's not only tolerated but also promoted in nearly every aspect of our society.

I know what you're saying: "Football's different." As the book *League of Denial: The NFL, Concussions, and the Battle for Truth* points out, in 2009 the NFL was warned by Boston University researcher Dr. Ann McKee that brain trauma was a very real—and very widespread—consequence of playing the game.

Am I to believe this is the only health warning given to a major employer that's ever been stubbornly downplayed or even ignored? Dr. McKee's testimony is obviously something that could have been discounted by a field dominated by ego-driven men. No question about that, just as a woman on Wall Street warning of an impending crash would be ignored out of male-dominated arrogance.

But for the sake of argument, let's say that the NFL suppressed legitimate medical evidence to protect its business. Fine. You win.

By all means, pay out millions—or even billions—to any football player who was shielded from medical evidence that showed his profession to be dangerous and even life threatening. Get out the checkbook if you ever knowingly suppressed or omitted clear and fact-based evidence that inarguably harmed a free safety. But let's not omit this, either: the medical field is ever changing. Even findings that are accepted as absolute truth are sometimes disproven decades later, and the brain—with its thirty billion neurons, give or take—is the most complex organ in our bodies.

Even the two doctors who recommended Accutane to me all those years ago had differing opinions on the drug's possible side effects.

Let's also remember this: the NFL is a league of football players, football coaches, and football executives. It's not a league of neurosurgeons. The league and its teams employ doctors and specialists, but is it possible that most of those doctors don't have expertise in brain trauma and don't have the time or inclination to pursue it?

Now let's reduce this to a more personal discussion about consumption and choice. From working on an oil rig because it pays well, to knocking down shots of tequila because they go down well, how much of his own actions is the individual responsible for in this age of information?

Football players, by the very definition of the sport, are adrenaline-seeking, testosterone-fueled risk takers. At two separate celebrity golf events, I watched former Chicago Bears quarterback Jim McMahon treat his body like an $18-a-day rental car. The fact that he downed a dozen beers before noon on both occasions was really none of my business until he joined a class-action lawsuit to sue the league. At that point, the story became a big part of my business.

Legitimate questions crop up. Are all of his postfootball physical issues NFL-related, or is it possible that some of them are lifestyle-related? How do we pinpoint the cause of McMahon's diagnosis of early-onset dementia? How did he treat his body on the 364 days of the year I *didn't* watch him? He has blasted the league for not providing "appropriate care," but did he provide "appropriate care" for himself all those years?

Yes, I know the statistics. I know the broken lives. I know a handful of NFL players have committed suicide. I also know dentists and veterinarians have a higher incidence of suicide than pro football players. Nearly every profession with alarmingly high suicide rates requires firearms as part of the job. Eight of the ten states with the highest rates don't even have NFL teams. For the most part, they're states with harsh winters.

That said, write a huge check to the family of Dave Duerson, a former Bears player who committed suicide in 2011. He was a thoughtful man who wanted his brain donated to research so that doctors such as McKee could gather more information on the incidence and effect of brain trauma in football players. I want those answers, too.

We all fight for more information. We fight for our rights of personal expression and freedom, fights that can't happen without taking risks. We are warned about alcohol but would lie and steal to obtain it. We are warned about firearms but demand the right to own them.

But I can't help but go back to that summer day in that dank Washington State Park bathroom, where I stood in stupefied amazement and looked at a pimple-free face staring back at me from a scuffed metal mirror. What those pills provided wasn't just a clear complexion but confidence and a more optimistic future. That might be overly dramatic, but I was seventeen and a dreamer like every other seventeen-year-old. In fact, it's just about the age that high school football players begin to get recruited for the next level. You know the one: it's one step from the NFL.

If any player walked blindly into the potential risks of an NFL career, write him a check. If any player played the game only because he believed lies he was told, write him a check.

But many of those players will cash those checks knowing a deeper truth.

Football is and always was a choice littered with physical risks. But what it gave those men was the same thing a daily dose of Accutane gave me. At that age and in that moment, they got to live a life they couldn't duplicate without it.

# WHEN OFFERED
## DELICOUS NACHOS
# AFTER 11:00 P.M.,
## AS A MAN YOU SAY
# "YES" AND "THANK YOU."
## YOU WORRY ABOUT THE
# RAMIFICATIONS LATER.

# THE LUCKY SON

**M**Y MOM AND I were having a casual conversation about family one day several years ago, when, out of nowhere, she said the following:

"It was so sweet of your father to write a check to pay his mother's bills over the last decade of her life."

I promise you, swear to God, she said this without an ulterior motive. There was nothing passive-aggressive in her tone or her timing. She was just stating a fact: it *was* sweet of my father to take care of his mother's financial obligations in her final years. We should all be so lucky to have a child so generous.

More than most mothers, mine wasn't engineered to seek pity. She bolted England when she was fourteen, leaving behind a tough childhood that included abuse. She jumped onto a ship with another young friend, and together they headed for New

York City. When I was fourteen, I was still afraid to sleep with the lights off. My mom was getting on a ship and leaving her entire world behind. She remembered the one Christmas during her childhood when she received an orange—a single, solitary orange—and felt thankful for it. When I became an adult, finally able to look at her and her life through adult eyes, I told her the greatest gift she gave me was her fierce self-reliance.

Her offhand comment about my dad stayed with me, and about ten years later, with my career rounding into shape, I called her.

After the usual small talk, I said, "Hey, Mom, how much are your monthly bills?"

"I'm fine, honey," she said. "I've never missed a payment of any kind in my life."

"That's not what I asked."

She tried to put me off, but I persisted until I got the number. From that month until she died, it was the easiest check I ever wrote. I stopped counting the number of times she thanked me at roughly 2,651.

I tell the story because it leads up to an even better story. Sitting around a crackling fire pit after a summer salmon bake in tiny Grayland, Washington, roughly ten years after I wrote that first check, someone suggested we head down the road and do some gambling at a small local casino.

Immediately, before anyone else could answer, my mom said, "Oh, that sounds fun. I win almost every time I go."

My brow furrowed. I did a little double take.

"*Really?*" I asked. "How often do you go?"

"Oh, at least twice a week. Maybe more."

Hmmm. I was doing the math in my head, trying to contain my surprise at this news.

"You do?" I said. "I didn't know you were such a big gambler."

She laughed a little, as if to say there was a lot about her I didn't know.

"Where do you get the money?" I asked.

With the warmth of a proud and loving mother, she said, "Well, you send me some every month, honey."

"But Mom, I thought you really needed that money."

And with that, my eighty-year-old mother raised her chin just a touch, did a quick scan of the assembled faces around the fire pit, and said:

"I do . . . for gambling."

Oh, if you could have heard the laughter that followed that line. It pierced the night. She passed several months later, and our evening around the fire pit was the last quality time we had together. At her funeral, I thought how fitting it was that this wonderful woman—sly and sharp to the very end—would never stop delivering for others.

That just had to be her last line:

"I do . . . for gambling."

And with that, she dropped the mic and walked off the stage.

Maybe directly into a casino.

# LETTER OF INTENT

Dear Sports Gods,

First things first, fellas: your work these last couple of years has been just awesome. Really well done. I'm especially fond of the messages you've been sending with your recent championships. Most people probably didn't notice, but I did. I see you working. Like all mystical beings, you operate in subtle and mysterious ways, but by about the third one, I could sense the pattern. You rewarded all the best coaches with titles. Coach K got one. So did Urban Meyer with Ohio

State. Gregg Popovich with the Spurs,
Bill Belichick, Bruce Bochy—I couldn't
have been the only one who was onto
you guys, could I? The best coaches in
each sport ended up holding the biggest
trophies, and from what I can tell, you
guys aren't big on coincidence. (Look, I
know: people might argue about whether
those guys are the best, and there's
been a necessary re-examination of
Belichick since Deflategate, but what
are you going to do? We're only human.)
You're spreading a righteous gospel:
coaching—and by extension, parenting or
mentoring—matters. God only knows (oops—
the name-in-vain faux pas; always been a
problem) how I appreciate that message.
My wife and I have more kids than Brad
and Angelina, so what matters to us is
not just that there's a winner but who
that winner is.

I also like the players you chose to
lead these teams. They're good people
and hardworking athletes, and some
of them are even willing to take pay
cuts for the good of the team. Guys
like Tim Duncan and Hunter Pence—real

beatitude guys, if you ask me. I know
you've never been obvious about showing
your hand—although Seattle throwing
that interception at the goal line came
awfully close to violating that rule—
but it's cool that you've always kept
the championships away from the Stephon
Marburys and Johnny Manziels. A slip-up
here and there, and people might lose
faith, if you know what I mean. And I
think you do.

Sometimes, though, you do things that
confound me. I mean, I'm not really sure
what to think of University of Kentucky
basketball coach John Calipari. He won
big once, but those big wins were vacated
at the University of Massachusetts
because Marcus Camby took $40,000 from
an agent, and at Memphis because someone
took the SAT for Derrick Rose. But
now he's winning big again by taking
full advantage of college basketball's
revolving-door, one-and-done philosophy.
The only thing I can figure is that
you guys have decided to empower the
players, and I guess I can't argue with
that message, either. Why should young

basketball stars be treated differently
than young stars in other entertainment
fields? I suppose it's one of those do-
unto-others moments that you guys feel
so strongly about. And you're right:
Sometimes we all need that reminder.

One of the things I've appreciated,
especially recently, is how you've
managed to spread the wealth. Least
of my brethren, right? The Lakers and
Yankees had their runs, but you yanked
that rug out, and now both of those
franchises, under the apathetic eye of
their second-generation Lucky Sperm
Club owners, are raging tire fires.
Do gods wink? Because right now, I've
got a feeling you guys are sending one
my way. As a sign of your mercy and
compassion, you've energized long-
suffering Seattle fans and made a whole
bunch of people in the Midwest rid
themselves of their long-held belief
that they're just flyover folks who are
ignored and ostracized by both coasts.
You've brought consistent excellence to
the Packers, and you dropped Andrew Luck
into Indianapolis like manna from you-

know-where. And at the risk of laying it on a bit too heavy, you delivered Jim Harbaugh from one of those chichi centers of urbanity to the University of Michigan, right about the time Wolverines fans were wondering if they'd ever matter again.

But you didn't stop there. Bo Ryan, a guy who looks like he should be flashing his badge and taking notes outside a murder scene in Boston, has created a basketball powerhouse in Madison, Wisconsin. Same for the Cardinals in St. Louis. And then, as the miracle to top all miracles, you made the Kansas City Royals interesting once again. Tip of the cap to you on that one, guys. I can only imagine the high fives that went around the room when one of you proposed that one.

That's not to say we don't have our disagreements. You waited far too long to open America's eyes to the ugliness of domestic violence among athletes, even though it's been right in front of us for years. There are smaller quibbles, too, like the way you've

allowed money to be the driving force
behind too many players and teams,
and by the way that personal seat
licensing scam you allow in the NFL is
Bernie Madoff 2.0. And at the risk of
asking for too much, could you also do
something about the incessant television
time-outs during football games, and
drunk fans, and baseball announcers
who feel the need to dissect every
pitch, and the icing-the-kicker rule?
And if you've got any time after that,
maybe you could address the issue of
random dudes talking about either their
March Madness bracket or their fantasy
football team?

Don't get me wrong: overall, I love
what you're doing. Women now have more
opportunities than ever in sports. We're
finally examining some of the hypocrisy
of the NCAA—not surprising, since I know
hypocrisy is something of a specialty
with you guys. The fan experience gets
better every year. Information on the
risk and consequences of concussions is
readily available to athletes and their
parents. Chewing tobacco is virtually

gone in baseball, and hopefully Alex Rodriguez will be, too.

You know, guys, sometimes I feel like I have to explain us mere mortals to you. From your vantage point, some of this obsession we have for our games might look a little silly. But I want you to know that sports makes us cry, and it makes us think, and sometimes we take it too seriously—after all, you warned us about false gods—but it creates a community where we cheer and root together in a world that's often splintered and divided. More than anything, it makes us feel like we're all a part of something, together. And take it from me: that matters.

So thanks.
Colin Cowherd

PS: Is it possible LeBron could win two more titles?

# AFTERWORD

IT WAS A COLD CONNECTICUT SATURDAY, and during the long winter of 2014–15, you could be forgiven for believing there would never be any other kind. My eight-year-old son and I were spending the weekend together. I made his favorite pancakes for breakfast and helped him with a school reading assignment after that. He was putting on his basketball uniform, which I had washed and laid out for him hours earlier, when he said something that stopped me in my tracks:

"I love you, Dad," he said. "All you have done all day is help me."

My sacrifice is no greater than any other parent's, but my son's words—and my feeling upon hearing them—revealed a universal truth: It's just what you do as a dad. It's what you *want* to do as a dad. You are selfless without thinking about it, and selfless without wanting credit.

It would be absurd to expect the same type of consideration from a fellow employee, especially in a bottom-line business like the media. Everyone has his or her own concerns: a family, a personal brand, a future.

That's why working once again with Tim Keown on a book project is so special. And so hard to put into words.

How do you explain the value of working with someone who is so selfless he would undoubtedly be embarrassed by the very credit I would give him? How do you explain the kind of talent that allows someone to take a nuanced, personal story I toiled over for days and return it—an hour later, believe it or not—so polished it gives me goose bumps?

There are so many people with talent in this world, and yet so few that have it but don't seek the attention that would surely benefit them.

When you find someone like that—and I should correct that: *if*, not *when*—make sure you tell him, again and again, how valuable he is. He won't seek it. It's not in his nature.

But saying thank you is in everyone's.

# ACKNOWLEDGMENTS

**I** **WOULD LIKE TO TAKE A MOMENT** to acknowledge the people who assisted me in writing my second book, but first I'd like to acknowledge something about my acknowledgments: the list may seem a bit random. I won't apologize, though, because the randomness is perfectly in keeping with my life. Through the eight divorces my parents had between the two of them, through me living in all four corners of this fine country, to the six kids—in blended families—that are now part of my life, there's not much order to be found. But that's okay. I wouldn't have it any other way. And did I mention I'm now moving everyone across the country once more, this time to Los Angeles?

If I were to forsake randomness for completeness, the list of those to whom I owe a debt of gratitude would be too damned long and unwieldy. I mean, tell me the truth—do you really want to hear about an incredibly supportive broadcasting professor, a man named David Terwische, who predicted all this would happen someday and demanded that I believe it, too? Do you want to hear about Mike Cutler, who surrendered to my persistent pleading and handed me my first broadcasting job despite my complete and utter lack of experience? There's also Bruce Gilbert, who had the courage to hire me at ESPN even though the television execs preferred hiring a more familiar *SportsCenter* voice, or at least a major-market radio host.

Do you want to hear about the instincts of my literary agent, Richard Abate, who became a vegan during the time I wrote this book and now actually calls me back on occasion? Who knew all those beans could hold so much power? I could also spend a few lines thanking the fine folks who edited this book, Jeremie Ruby-Strauss and Nina Cordes. They work in New York, and for the life of me, I can't recall working with people who were better with punctuation. Damn, do they ever know their way around a comma.

God, this is tedious, right?

I left out several hundred people in this brief post-game recap, but someone I can't ignore is my radio producer, Vince Kates, who has somewhere between five and thirteen children and yet somehow does everything from book my travel to deliver daily gems used on the air. He even shielded me from management when I offended an advertiser by mocking its product on the air. That, ladies and gentleman, is a true friend.

Oh, and since I have a voracious sexual appetite, I'd like to acknowledge my stunning and sexy wife, Ann. No, wait, that sounds wrong. She's hot . . . wait . . . let me back this thing up. My wife, Ann, is funny and smart and full of wisdom and supports me in my darkest hours. She tells me things I don't want to hear, and isn't it strange how those things, in hindsight, are exactly the things I needed to hear?

The truth is, I'd like to acknowledge an overriding truth: I've arrived at a place in life that is exactly what I've hoped for. It's filled with laughter and support and just enough angst to keep it interesting. Most of all, though, it's filled with people who allow me the freedom to pursue my dreams.

Family dreams. Professional dreams.

And that part isn't random at all.